V/STOL

THE KEY TO SURVIVAL

Roy Braybrook

V/STOL

THE KEY TO SURVIVAL

OSPREY

Dedication

This book is dedicated to the next generation of novelty salesmen.
May they find the success that eluded mine. RB.

Published in 1989 by Osprey Publishing Limited
59 Grosvenor Street, London W1X 9DA

British Library Cataloguing in Publication Data

Braybrook, Roy
    V/STOL: the key to survival.
    1. North Atlantic Treaty Organization air forces.
    Use of vertical/short take-off and landing aeroplane-proposals.
    I. Title
    358.4′03′091821

ISBN 0-85045-767-X

Editor Dennis Baldry
Designed by Martin Bronkhorst
Printed in Great Britain by Butler and Tanner Ltd, Frome, Somerset

Contents

Foreword

In peacetime military men and their political masters are generally cautious and conservative. Doctrines and philosophies of operation and deployment, distilled from the perceived wisdoms of past war successes and leavened by (usually over-estimated) appreciations of what a potential adversary can do, become embodied like holy writ in the manuals, practices and training of a fighting service. This has been so for several past centuries; indeed such an approach is perhaps in the very nature of such large complex organizations as navies, armies and air forces.

But in war the triumphs and victories go usually to those who exercise and practice the unconventional, the swift and flexible, the responsive and the unpredictable: in tactics, in methods, and in equipment.

Tactical airpower used in support of land forces and in fleets of ships at sea became, in two world wars, the supreme example of these military virtues. Mobile tactical airpower as practiced by the Third Reich changed the face of Europe in the early 1940s and, exercised by the Allies, changed it again in the mid-1940s. Mobile seaborne tactical airpower was a chief instrument in both the establishment and dismemberment of the Japanese 'Greater Asian Co-Prosperity Sphere' in the 1940s.

From 1940, in Europe, the Maginot Line became the symbol for an outmoded defence posture. Yet today, some 45 years on from the introduction into service of the first jets, the deployment of

This trio of Egyptian Air Force MiG-21s was caught in the open by an Israeli strafing run during the pre-emptive strikes of the 1967 Six-Day War. (*Keystone*)

tactical airpower has developed into the contemporary equivalent of France's supposed-impregnable Maginot defences.

An overwhelming proportion of NATO's tactical airpower depends in war on the continuing availability of peacetime bases with long runways. We need to think of such 2,500 to 3,500 metre concrete pads, with their surrounding infrastructure and defences, as Maginot type 'fortresses.' There are, maybe, only a hundred or two such military runways available from the North Cape to the Turkish end of our NATO frontier. If you include civil runways, the number may double. But it is sickeningly finite. A thrust west by Warsaw Pact forces doesn't have to eliminate *all* these runways—only those located so that their squadrons can contest the sector under threat. The position of every runway is known to an accuracy of metres. We can't hide them: we can't move them, nor their associated support complexes: we cannot completely defend them—certainly not against determined saturation attacks nor even against moderate-range surface-to-surface missiles dispensing a wicked armoury of cratering weapons, mines of all types, or chemical agents.

Our tactical aircraft and their pilots and ground crews may mostly survive in perimeter-scattered hardened shelters. But they are extremely unlikely to be able to contribute to the fighting in the critical areas, where the combat aircraft can make its best impact. In fact, many of our finest hi-tech CTOL aircraft have a high probability of being preserved by the victor as future shiny museum-pieces—in mint condition, only one previous owner; as the brochure might say!

This same Maginot-type fortress doctrine has even become the norm for seaborne tactical airpower. The mass of naval tactical air capability is tied today to a relative handful of large, vulnerable, high value, unconcealable, mobile bases that we know as the CTOL aircraft carrier. In times of need there will never be sufficient such ships. Because of their high value, much of their enormous offensive air capability will be dissipated in the vital interests of their own self-defence—even if the command chooses not to send them forward into areas of high threat. The lessons of two world wars have shown the vulnerability of Europe's Atlantic lifeline to the absence of continuous and preferably integral naval airpower in defence of such vital sea lanes.

As a shelterer under the NATO shield I keep on asking myself, and others, when are we going to take seriously those so-evident weaknesses in the deployment of our tactical airpower?

War is full of surprises. The known and predictable—and the immobile—are always the more easily countered by a flexible, audacious and aggressive adversary. Surprise, mobility, concentration and flexibility have always been key factors for success in war.

There exists today, and for the past two decades or so, a means to overcome many of the inherent liabilities and weaknesses of CTOL tactical aviation. It is the V/STOL aircraft. It's greatest sin is that it is perceived as a threat by the overwhelming majority of the senior airmen who command our tactical CTOL aviation fleets and those who direct our future plans. V/STOL is regarded as a threat in my belief, because it upsets the status quo: because for its proper exploitation the entire method of operation of land and sea-based tactical aviation and its effective deployment has to be rethought. The military machine is large and has enormous self-perpetuating momentum. We all—not only military men—prefer to think along routine, established, comfortable (and comforting) channels. Resistance to change is one of the most persistent of human traits, particularly in the older sectors of our population; those men we select and charge with governing our affairs and destiny, whether civilian or military.

The only two powered lift tactical jets in service today, the West's Harriers and the Soviet's Yak-38 *Forger*, are not new. Harrier soon will complete its second decade of service with the RAF. The *Forger* has been around, visible to western cameras on the high seas, for 12 years. Five 'Western' air arms fly Harrier—three of them primarily from small ships at sea.

What do we need further to prove that the V/STOL concept is practical, competitive and economical: both on land and at sea? We who fathered and nurtured Kingston's unique Jump-Jet used to wish, anguishedly, for a convenient small war where the Harrier could prove its so-evident merits. Well, we had one in 1982. It was called the Falklands. And what was the response of the doubters and CTOL-ists to the unequalled contribution of the RAF and RN Harriers to that campaign? 'Ah' they said: 'It was special. It happened at short notice' (when will we ever be given 'long' notice?!) They go on: 'It won't happen again. It doesn't apply in NATO.' To crown all such comments there was also the post-war study that forcefully pointed out how much better and quicker the UK would have completed the job using a couple of *Nimitz*-size ships with AEW, etc . . . There are no prizes for guessing who 'proved' that conclusion!

Sadly, the Falklands campaign did not markedly change the demand for V/STOL fish in the aviation procurement fishmarkets of the world. The US Marine Corps, from whose pride in the advantages of V/STOL and their endless extolling of its virtues, you could believe they alone invented both the concept and configuration, are also regarded by other air arms around the world, because of their amphibious assault role, as a 'special case.' So they are, and deservedly so, too. Hence the published benefits from their V/STOL experience go largely ignored because of military myopia concerning the USMC's special role, despite the more general military applicability of the Marines' experience with Harrier on land and at sea.

The Band of Brothers who have espoused the jet V/STOL cause continues growing. But far too slowly for the risk entailed. The CTOL heathen still resist stoutly from the illusory ramparts of their Maginot-like fortresses on land and at sea. Change is slow to effect: existing momentum and investment in CTOL tactical aviation is massive. The new and allegedly unknown (—after a million V/STOL operating flight hours round the world!!) apparently is more feared than is the trauma consequent upon admitting that our present CTOL postures are at root untenable and at the very best entail high risk of failing to deliver when the chips are down.

But technology still cometh. The first practical supersonic V/STOL tactical aircraft need only money to give them physical substance. Collectively, the present defence development community seems determined to research them into stillbirth. Perhaps when grandson-of-P.1154 lifts off in the 1990s—an eminently practicable goal—the air arms of the world will find reason to change doctrinal course, both on land and at sea. My oft-repeated offer to fit a two-to-one geared Machmeter hasn't significantly increased the market for today's Harriers.

V/STOL is not a cure for all tactical aviation ailments. But it doesn't today operate at a penalty compared with an *equivalent* CTOL attack fighter. CTOL will still comprise a large segment of our 21st century tactical airfleets. But we *must*—and *now*—start to direct a far more significant fraction of our development and procurement efforts and funds into v/STOL. The prizes are there to be grasped and exploited by the militarily bold and eager—continued survival on land, flexibility of operation in all weathers and terrains, independence of known fixed bases, and the promise of a continuing concealed mobile threat when most of our CTOL airpower is negated. At sea, naval airpower can be extended into many ships in a fleet;—smaller ships, more affordable ships and even into merchant-type ships. Sea control without adequate numbers of sea bases for tactical naval aircraft is a maritime myth.

The challenge is not predominantly technical nor logistical, nor even in areas of command and control. It seems still that the obstacles we must overcome are largely doctrinal.

I hope that this book will contribute to increasing success in this campaign. Roy Braybrook, like myself, has spent the majority of his professional working life developing and championing the v/STOL cause. Most of the seeds we have sown over the past 30 years have fallen on barren ground. I hope the seeds from this work will germinate over a wider area of fertile ground, and thus facilitate the earlier reaping of a harvest of defence effectiveness that is long and distressingly overdue.

Dr John W Fozard
Washington, DC
January 1989

Dr John W Fozard, OBE, FEng, FRS, FRAeS.
Dr John W Fozard has spent some 45 years in the aerospace industry, the past 30 of them deeply concerned with and committed to jet v/STOL. Having been appointed Chief Designer of the Hawker P.1154 in 1963 he became (after that aircraft was cancelled in 1965) Chief Designer, Harrier, from 1965 to 1978 with Hawker Siddeley Aviation. He continued at British Aerospace, Kingston, as Marketing Director for Harrier and Hawk to 1984, thereafter being Divisional Director Special Projects in the Military Aircraft Division of BAe. He currently occupies the prestigious Lindbergh Chair of Aerospace History at the Smithsonian Institution's National Air and Space Museum in Washington, DC.

Preface

A BAe Harrier GR.3 of No 4 Sqn, RAF Germany, lands vertically at a dispersed site. (Crown copyright)

High performance aircraft capable of v/STOL (vertical or short take-off and landing) represent a unique category in the broad spectrum of recent aviation developments. Only v/STOL aircraft can provide the dispersal capability that guarantees the survival of a nation's airpower in the face of intensive attacks on airfields. Only v/STOL can make possible military deployments in any part of the world, regardless of airfield availability. In the naval context, only v/STOL aircraft make it feasible for the less wealthy nations to possess fixed-wing maritime air capability through the use of mini-carriers, and for the more wealthy nations to disperse their naval air assets and thus minimize the possible effects of the loss of any one ship. In civil use, only v/STOL aircraft make possible city-centre operations, and thus the prospect of rapid transit between city pairs.

Taking the broad view of v/STOL, it is clear that in principle such aircraft offer major operational attractions for both military and civil users. However, it is equally obvious that there is a wide gulf between this principle and current practice. The v/STOL aircraft appear to be gaining ground slowly against conventional (CTOL) aircraft in naval terms, if the balance is judged in terms of the number of services operating either type. On the other hand, in terms of actual numbers of aircraft the advantage is still overwhelmingly with CTOL, the US Navy alone having some 1,500 CTOL combat aircraft.

Britain's RAF is the only air force so far to have adopted V/STOL (the US Marine Corps being effectively a special duties branch of the US Navy), and Harriers still make up only a fraction of the RAF's combat arm. For the time being (at least) the idea of high performance V/STOL commercial transports has been abandoned, due to intractable noise problems and high costs. The tilt-rotor, or the X-Wing may ultimately revive it, but this remains to be seen.

The V/STOL aircraft is thus something of a paradox. In principle it appears to have real advantages for military, naval and civil operators, yet in almost 30 years it has made only proportionally microscopic inroads into the global aircraft market. Assuming that aircraft are purchased on a rational basis (which is another interesting topic for discussion), this situation might be taken to indicate that V/STOL aircraft are perceived to have some major practical disadvantages. In fact there were several other factors involved in what can only be regarded as a marketing disaster, including national pride, the absence of high level support for the concept (before the advent of Margaret Thatcher), the lack of suitable endorsement in the form of a major overseas operator such as the USAF or the German Air Force, and the arguably mistaken belief that a V/STOL purchase made nonsense of older CTOL aircraft within the service.

This category of aircraft is also unique in the sense that V/STOL is the only significant branch of recent aviation progress in which Britain has achieved a world lead. The fact that the Harrier aircraft and its Pegasus engine derive from a French idea and owed a great deal to US funding in their early stages can be (and is) glossed over and forgotten. For all practical purposes, the Harrier-Pegasus combination is totally British, and throughout the 1970s and early 1980s was years ahead of any other nation's V/STOL projects. One day it may be regretted in this country that the decision was taken in Whitehall not to spend the money required to maintain what was our only significant aviation lead.

In this book I have attempted to discuss both the operational case for V/STOL and the various factors that have militated against its acceptance. The book also discusses the mistakes that were made in developing (or in attempting unsuccessfully to develop) V/STOL aircraft, and what should be done in the West to keep abreast of possible Soviet developments in this field.

This book may not supply all the answers of V/STOL, but I would hope that it provides the general reader with some useful information on which to base his opinions on this subject. From my own quarter-century of experience in the design and marketing of v/STOL combat aircraft, I would certainly argue that v/STOL deserves to be represented in a far greater slice of military aviation than is currently the case. Any major air arm that faces the threat of strikes against its bases should have a v/STOL element to ensure survival.

It seems likely that v/STOL will achieve the status it deserves only when the advantages it offers and the limitations of CTOL and STOL aircraft are more widely appreciated. It is my hope that this book will contribute to this understanding.

Roy Braybrook,
Ashtead, Surrey 1989

1

A Real Operational Need but Few Sales

The Growth of Airpower

One of the main features of the development of warfare in the 20th Century has been the growth in importance of airpower at the expense of that exercised by armies and navies.

At the time of World War 1 aeroplanes were lightweight vehicles with little real military value aside from tactical reconnaissance. The fighting scouts may have provided the aces that distracted the public attention from the slaughter in the muddy trenches, and both aeroplanes and airships brought the risk of sudden death to civilians in hitherto safe rear areas, but airpower remained a peripheral activity. The outcome of the conflict had to be decided on the surface of the Earth, not in the skies above it.

By the time of the Spanish Civil War airpower had become a terror weapon, a means to destroy undefended cities, and thus to strike directly at one's opponent's will to continue the fight. The advent of radar (initially restricted to ground stations, though later developed in airborne form) made it possible for Britain to provide an effective air defence system for its cities and major military installations by 1940, though in daylight only.

As the pendulum swung in favour of the Allies, Germany was forced to develop a multi-layered day/night air defence system, but the overall advantage remained with the night bombers, which laid waste whole cities in an attempt to deprive German industrial

Operating conditions off the Falklands were appalling, but a very high level of availability was maintained, thanks to the ships' crews, who worked extremely hard and showed considerable ingenuity with their aircraft protection schemes. (MoD)

workers of their homes. However, it was only with the dropping of the atomic bombs on Hiroshima and Nagasaki on the 6th and 9th of August 1945 that airpower finally achieved a war-winning status. Suddenly, a single aircraft could incinerate thousands of unprepared civilians, and the nature of war would never be the same again.

By the 1960s the manned aircraft had lost something of its importance, since its role in delivering nuclear warheads was being taken over by intercontinental and submarine-launched ballistic missiles (ICBMS and SLBMS) against which there was no real defence. On the other hand, the advent of small nuclear weapons had given aircraft a much larger influence on the outcome of the surface battle. They might still be limited in their ability to destroy the enemy infantryman or tank at the forward edge of the battle area (FEBA), but they could very effectively interdict the supplies essential to continued fighting, and they could prevent second-echelon units reinforcing or replacing those in the front line.

Today the ballistic missile may be the ultimate weapon, but the use of nuclear warheads gives the manned aircraft a vitally important role in the land and sea battles, as well as in deep strikes into enemy territory.

Current Limitations

The growth in the significance of airpower is widely recognized, though armies are still needed to occupy territory, and navies are still essential to protect sea lines of communication (SLOCS). What is less generally appreciated is that despite the technological progress that has made possible very high speeds, long ranges and heavy payloads, the manned aircraft is left with some serious shortcomings.

For example, aircraft still provide only a very limited logistics effort in comparison with surface transport, and it is quite possible that this situation will never change. Aeroplanes are a good way to move (say) a division of troops and most of their essential equipment if speed is vitally important, but they cannot substitute for ships and trains when it comes to moving whole armies and thousands of tanks. It used to be said that for each ton of high-priority equipment that a USAF transport delivered to Vietnam, an old-fashioned ship had to deliver a ton of fuel to get the aircraft back to the States again.

A second basic factor restricting the practical value of the manned aircraft is that the technology required to achieve today's high speeds has led to a severe dependence on large, vulnerable operating bases. Even as recently as WW2, fighters could operate from grass fields. Early Soviet jet fighters (up to and including the MiG-21) can operate from specially improved grass areas on either side of the standard Warsaw Pact runway. In the West, only the v/stol Harrier can operate from grass, but in wartime it would use paved surfaces to ensure a continuous capability.

High speeds have been achieved not simply by applying more power, but by using proportionally smaller wings (i.e., high wing loadings) and increasingly high packaging densities. As aircraft density has increased, tyres pressures have been forced upward to restrict tyre size. Since the days of the Hurricane and Spitfire, combat aircraft tyre pressures have shot up by a factor of around 10. With these high pressures has come the need for a thick paved operating surface, without which the modern fighter is useless.

As wing loadings have increased, stall speeds have risen, and with them landing distances. Take-off distances have suffered less in this respect, since high thrust/weight ratios have improved acceleration to unstick speed. Nonetheless, the overall result is that a modern combat aircraft operates from a concrete runway that is typically 8,000 ft (2,500 m) long and around 10 inches (25 cm) thick, and that from the air can be seen for miles. If the enemy can make two cuts in the concrete, that fighter probably cannot land at its own base. After four runway cuts, it can probably take off only in an air defence configuration, or to escape at reduced weight to another airfield.

In essence, the main thrust of fighter development has been to increase speed virtually regardless of penalties in other areas. Instead of taking a broad view of how the aircraft is to survive not only in flight but also on the ground, we have produced a vehicle that is magnificent in the air, but totally dependent on its runway remaining intact.

In this sense the fighter is as fundamentally vulnerable as the Maginot Line was in the 1930s. France's defences were completely dependent on Germany making a frontal assault on her fortified positions. The usefulness of the modern combat aircraft is completely dependent on its airfield not being attacked successfully. In May 1940 Germany broke the rules and attacked France through neutral Belgium and the supposedly impenetrable forest of the Ardennes, outflanking the Maginot Line. What if tomorrow the Warsaw Pact refuses to play the game, and attacks NATO airfields?

Misleading Experience

It is arguable that the vulnerability of the modern NATO fighter to airfield attack is largely the result of American experience. Since 1947 (when the F-86 Sabre first flew) the US has led the world in fighter development, and Europe has tended to accept without serious questioning whatever line the designers on the other side of the Atlantic have chosen to adopt. In most respects this unquestioning acceptance of American standards has worked to NATO's advantage. In fairness it must also be added that in some respects Europe has ploughed its own furrow, as in the case of aircraft handling qualities and in gun armament. However, in tyre pressures and wing loadings we have followed the Americans, and with one exception we have ended up with fighters that are just as dependent on their runways remaining intact. A particular set of historical circumstances has led US combat aircraft development into a trap, and most designers in Europe have followed mindlessly behind.

The fact is that for more than 40 years American forces have taken supremacy in the air for granted, hence the vulnerability of US operating bases to air attack has not been a matter for serious concern. Whenever Harrier salesmen tried to interest USAF officers in the V/STOL concept, the invariable response was that the ability to operate despite runway bombing was unnecessary, since no-one ever bombed USAF runways. '*For that to happen we would have had to have lost air superiority, and without air superiority we would have lost the war anyway*' was the attitude often encountered.

The officers concerned were not morons. They were merely summarising the lessons of four decades of practical experience. Once the Japanese onslaught had run out of steam and America had rearmed, the only air attacks to which US surface targets were vulnerable were *kamikaze* dives, the seriousness of which was restricted by standing patrols and proximity-fused AAA. By the time that US forces were heavily engaged in Europe, Germany's *Luftwaffe* was running out of fuel and experienced pilots. Some of the highest kill-ratios ever recorded were achieved in the later stages of the war in Europe, and it is hardly surprising that US air bases were seldom subjected to serious air attacks.

In the Korean War of 1950–53, Sabre pilots claimed 792 MiG-15 *Fagots* destroyed in the air for the loss of 78 of their own aircraft, hence a fair degree of air superiority was assured. Communist air attacks against USAF airfields played little part in the conflict, although small numbers of USAF aircraft made strafing attacks in the very early days, and one Chinese twin-piston Tu-2 *Bat* bomber was later shot down. The Tu-2 were later replaced by twin-jet Il-28 *Beagles*, which might in principle have constituted something of a night-time threat. However, fear of US reprisals gave UN bases freedom from bombing attacks. Provided that Chinese aircraft did not attack south of the 38th Parallel, it was decided by the Joint Chiefs of Staff that USAF bombers would not hit Chinese bases north of the Yalu River. To this extent Korea was a phoney war, yet it played a major role in the development of USAF tactical philosophy.

The Vietnam War lasted much longer, with the US involved from 1961 (though on a major scale only from 1965) until 1975. However, once again US airfields were safe from air attack, although those in South Vietnam were on occasion subjected to mortar and rocket attacks by insurgents.

Large-scale US involvement was triggered by the Tonkin Gulf incident of August 1964, when North Vietnamese patrol boats attacked USN destroyers. Retaliatory strikes were initially limited to the area just north of the demilitarized zone (DMZ), but in February 1965 President Johnson authorized a bombing campaign ('Rolling Thunder') against North Vietnam, and the air war started in earnest. At the time of the Tonkin Gulf incident, the North Vietnamese had only 30 training aircraft, 50 transports, and four light helicopters. Two days after the incident around 30 MiG-15s and -17s (*Frescos*) were supplied by China to the Phuc Yen airbase, and in June 1965 further aircraft of these types arrived from the Soviet Union, bringing the fighter total to 70. At the end of that year the first MiG-21s (*Fishbeds*) arrived. By mid-1965 the North Vietnamese had five or six Il-28 bombers at Phuc Yen, but the emphasis remained on air defence around the capital of Hanoi and the port of Haiphong.

This emphasis was reflected in the location of airfields. The principal military bases were Phuc Yen and Kep, both near Hanoi, with Gia Lam near Hanoi and Cat Bi and Kien An near Haiphong used as dispersal airfields. These five bases were clearly sited to defend the main targets, but the enemy also had a paved runway at Dong Hoi, just north of the DMZ, which was assessed by the USAF as capable of supporting limited jet operations.

On the US side, the Navy had at least two carriers off the coast of Vietnam, one on the 'Yankee' station carrying out strikes on the North, while that on the 'Dixie' station supported the Marine Corps in the South. The USAF tactical aircraft operated mainly from Da Nang and Cam Ranh Bay in the Republic of Vietnam (RVN) and from Korat, Takhli, Ubon and Udorn in Thailand. The B-52s operated from U-Tapao in Thailand, and from Andersen AFB on Guam. Missions from the ultimate security of Guam took place over a radius in excess of 2,500 nm (4,600 km), but the fighter strikes were equally impressive in their class, covering a radius of 300–600 nm (550–1,100 km). All the attacks on the North were supported by flight refuelling.

As stated earlier, none of the US bases were subjected to air attack. Whereas in the Korean War they had been protected by a tacit understanding aimed at limiting escalation of the conflict, in this case the enemy lacked the resources to make such attacks.

In May 1967 airfields in the North were declared valid targets, and in that first month USAF fighters destroyed 26 MiGs on the ground. However, there was virtually nothing that the North Vietnamese could do in retaliation. The only paved runway close to the DMZ was at Dong Hoi, which is a modest 75 nm (140 km) from Da Nang. A handful of MiG-21s could have made rocket attacks on the target-enriched base at Da Nang, operating at night and at low level from Dong Hoi, but this base would clearly have been blown off the map the next day. Likewise, Il-28s based at Phuc Yen might have made night-time strikes against coastal bases in the South or against the carrier on the 'Yankee' station, but these would have brought retaliation on a massive scale.

In daylight such attacks on US air bases would probably have been suicidal, since radar cover over SE Asia was reasonably good, and US fighters had some measure of air superiority. Primary air defence radars were installed not only at Da Nang (code-name 'Panama') and Pleiku ('Peacock'), but also in Thailand at Nakhon Phanom ('Invert'), Ubon ('Lion') and Udorn ('Brigham'). Airborne radar coverage was provided by USAF EC-121D Big Eye and the more advanced EC-121M Rivet Top aircraft, and Navy E-2As.

The direction of US fighters by radar-equipped patrol aircraft was one of the principal factors responsible for the favourable kill-ratio. Overall, 184 MiGs were destroyed in the air (129 by the USAF and 55 by the USN and USMC) for the loss of 75 US fighters (60 USAF and 15 USN and USMC). It is worthy of note that the overall balance in Vietnam was much less in favour of the US than in Korea, despite the fact that many of the aircraft flown by the North were obsolescent. Of those destroyed, 92 were MiG-17s, 10 were MiG-19s and only 82 were MiG-21s.

If the US drew lessons from other conflicts, it was probably from the Middle East wars of 1967 and 1973. However, in neither case were the airfields of the 'friendlies' (i.e., the Israelis) attacked effectively. The *Heyl Ha'Avir* certainly sustained heavy losses in the early days of the 1973 conflict, in desperate efforts to halt thrusts by Syrian and Egyptian ground forces equipped with a new generation of surface-air missiles (SAMS), but the Israelis had no problems with attacks on their own operating bases.

The conflicts that have occurred during the professional lives of the officers that now head the USAF have thus provided a number of lessons, some of which have been completely misleading when viewed in the context of a war between NATO and the Warsaw Pact countries. Admittedly, experience in Korea and Vietnam has continually kept the USAF aware of the need for good air superiority fighters, and America is consequently well ahead of Britain and even France in this field. However, the fact that US air bases have not been threatened with air attack for more than 40 years, coupled with the fact that USAF aircraft have enjoyed a significant degree of air superiority over its adversaries during this period, has left the service with an arguably excessive confidence in the security of its airfields.

Airfield Denial

The vulnerability of modern combat aircraft to airfield denial operations is due not only to their total dependence on vast stretches of concrete but also to the growth in the effectiveness of airfield attack systems.

One of the ironies of air warfare is that the nuclear weapons that give manned aircraft their great significance have also provided from the 1960s a means whereby an entire operational wing can instantly be struck from the balance sheet. A single minimum-scale warhead offers the promise that every aircraft, every hangar and every shelter on the field will be vaporized, every man killed, and the entire area contaminated against further use.

Moreover, the elimination of a complete base and three squadrons of aircraft does not depend on escalation to nuclear weapons. A single surface-surface missile can now deliver sufficient chemicals to close down the base completely in a surprise attack, or to restrict operations severely if defensive preparations have been made.

At a much lower level of warfare, operations from an airfield can be stopped or restricted by making cuts across the paved surfaces. Traditionally, this had been done by dropping sticks of bombs in dive attacks, but this involves a heavy warload and an attack profile that gives a high attrition rate. New developments in the field of runway attack systems now promise to make it possible to cut a runway with a much smaller payload, released in a low level pass to minimize attrition.

To recapitulate, by the 1960s combat aircraft had developed to an impressive level, but they were totally dependent on their airfields remaining intact. Notwithstanding evidence provided by the wars in Korea and SE Asia, in which USAF bases remained free from attack, the means were available (or being developed) to destroy an airfield completely with nuclear weapons, to severely restrict operations with chemical weapons, or to temporarily halt operations by means of runway cuts using traditional explosives. Throughout the 1960s these cuts had to be made with conventional bombs in an attack technique that involved heavy losses, but several countries were already developing runway-attack systems that largely eliminated this problem.

Today a variety of nations are working to improve further the attacker's chance of survival by means of stand-off attack systems, using winged (and in some examples powered) submunition-dispeners, which will allow the attacking aircraft to remain outside the reach of the airfield defences.

Dispersal Means Survival
While airfield attack weapons have been advancing in a series of major steps, air defence systems have also been improving,

though there is no evidence from actual conflicts to suggest that the attacking aircraft would now be subject to an unacceptable level of attrition, i.e. a loss rate of the order of 10 per cent. For example, the average USAF loss rate in attack sorties in SE Asia for the period 1965–68 was only 4.1 per cent.

In recent years various statements have been made by high-ranking NATO officers, indicating that in the event of war the Warsaw Pact is expected to make massed attacks against the principal Allied tactical bases, on a scale chosen to ensure positive results while swamping airfield defences. There is no doubt that the forces of the Pact have thousands of ground attack aircraft available (in addition to surface-surface missiles), and that each aircraft can fly several sorties per day. It is also accepted that targets beyond the battle area are particularly attractive to the Communist air forces, since such objectives eliminate the problems of inter-service coordination, an area in which peacetime exercises have demonstrated that Pact forces frequently encounter problems. Little information is available on Soviet airfield attack systems, but it is generally taken that they lag only slightly behind those employed by the principal Western forces.

The idea that significant numbers of NATO main operating bases will continue operations despite this onslaught does not appear to be based on the belief that the number of Pact aircraft assigned to airfield attack will be restricted due to other priorities, that the airfield attack systems employed will be ineffective, or that the attacking aircraft will be decimated by our fighters and airfield defences. The general attitude seems to be that nuclear weapons will not be used in the initial days of the conflict, that the reduction in sortie rates associated with chemical attacks is merely something to be endured, and that cuts in runways can be repaired quickly.

It is questionable whether such an attitude really makes sense, and whether those responsible are not simply inventing arguments to justify adherence to the 'fortress-airfield' concept that was established in the 1960s, when the threat of airfield attacks was less serious than it is today.

If a nation has spent vast sums to create and protect airbases, then it naturally requires unassailable evidence of the vulnerability of these bases before it abandons its fortress-airfields.

Switzerland is an excellent example of a country that has built mountain airfields. At considerable expense it has blasted caverns in the rock to house its aircraft, and has installed large numbers of automatic weapons to secure these wartime bases against air attack. It would be very difficult to persuade the Swiss to abandon this operational concept, although it can be argued that the cavern entrances may be attacked successfully with TV-guided weapons, that the runways are comparatively short, and that these airfields are equally vulnerable to chemical attacks.

However, NATO air bases are not really comparable to those of Switzerland. Our aircraft are housed in shelters that can be destroyed by a direct hit. Our airfield defences are proportionally less strong, representing only the final stage of a multi-layered defence. In terms of inflicting attrition on attacking aircraft, a great deal of the responsibility rests with the missile belts further forward and on air defence fighters. A change of operational philosophy would thus represent far less of a waste of valuable resources than in the Swiss case, although it might be seen as a loss of face for those who have backed the fortress-airfield concept.

Instead of finding arguments to justify adherence to what could well prove an outdated concept, NATO planners might logically take the view that our air assets are so numerically inferior to those of the Warsaw Pact that they must respond well in the widest possible spectrum of attack scenarios. These aircraft must not be pinned down for hours while runways are repaired. Their sortie rates must not be cut by chemical attacks. They must go on operating in the presence of tactical nuclear strikes.

The only way that aircraft can avoid the effects of nuclear and chemical attacks on main operating bases is to disperse to small sites that (even if they are detected) do not warrant the use of such warheads. The only way that aircraft can continue operations despite any conceivable level of runway destruction is by incorporating special features that enable them to use far shorter take-off and landing distances than is possible with conventional designs. In short, the only answer to the modern airfield attack threat is the V/STOL aircraft.

Other Advantages And Some Disadvantages

The V/STOL combat aircraft has other advantages in comparison with the conventional (CTOL) designs that now make up the vast majority of fighters and ground attack aircraft on both sides of the Iron Curtain. In the maritime context, v/STOL aircraft make possible high performance operations from relatively small ships, thus eliminating the possibility of a major loss of air assets in a single nuclear strike. The use of small carriers also facilitates a graduated response in brush-fire wars, and brings fixed-wing naval aviation within the grasp of less wealthy nations.

In land-based use, v/STOL aircraft make possible forward basing, with quick response times in the close support role, unprecedented sortie rates, and closer contact with the troops for whom the aircraft provide reconnaissance information and fire support. Such aircraft also have special attractions in a rapid deployment context, since they can operate in areas where conventional military bases are non-existent, and can leave civil airports free for the use of transport aircraft bringing in troops and supplies.

Some types of v/STOL aircraft have special advantages in close combat manoeuvres, due to their ability to deflect their propulsive jets in flight, and to maintain attitude control irrespective of airspeed. At present these features are employed purely in last-ditch defensive maneouvres, but more advanced v/STOL aircraft may further exploit this concept, e.g. in achieving acceleration in pitch beyond the capability of CTOL aircraft. However, some new STOL projects, notably the Lockheed YF-22A and Northrop YF-23A, will also feature in-flight thrust vectoring.

Whether or not v/STOL aircraft will prove in the long term to have a fundamental advantage in air combat manoeuvres, there is no doubt that their flexibility of basing offers significant attractions. This is particularly true for the operator faced with a powerful opponent, or that may have to deploy forces to regions with few conventional airbases. It is unquestionably true for a nation that needs fixed-wing aircraft at sea, but cannot afford conventional carriers. Whereas land-based v/STOL aircraft demonstrate superior cost-effectiveness only in wartime, their sea-based equivalents provide substantial savings in peacetime by operating from relatively low-cost ships.

The apparent basing advantages of v/STOL aircraft over their CTOL counterparts are so great that it is clear there must also be disadvantages (real or imaginary), otherwise the world's combat aircraft would long ago have made the switch to v/STOL.

There is no denying that v/STOL aircraft are somewhat less

straightforward to develop, and rather more expensive to produce and to operate than those in the CTOL category. However, it may be argued that, while it was convenient to make the first high performance V/STOL design a subsonic attack aircraft, this decision automatically led to a very large performance penalty. In this class the engine is sized conventionally (e.g., in the A-4 Skyhawk) merely to suit cruise thrust demands, and is thus relatively light, allowing a great deal of fuel to be carried. In designing such an aircraft for V/STOL performance, roughly twice as much thrust was required, warload-radius being severely penalized.

A modern fighter such as the F-16 requires a thrust greater than or (at least) equal to its clean take-off weight, hence a V/STOL fighter is much closer to its CTOL equivalent than is the case with a ground attack aircraft. If a V/STOL fighter can also avoid the Harrier's problem of requiring a special design of engine that cannot be used in other applications, then a further aspect of the V/STOL cost penalty will also have been eliminated.

The commercial success of the Harrier has certainly been limited by the fact that it is not a supersonic aircraft. The reason for this was that an engine of very high thrust/weight ratio was developed simply and cheaply by hanging a large fan on the front of an existing turbojet, producing a turbofan of comparatively high bypass ratio. This gave a great deal of thrust at low speeds for V/STOL, but as speed increased the thrust decayed rapidly. It is thus virtually impossible to design a supersonic aircraft around a 'dry' Pegasus.

However, there are no insuperable problems in designing a supersonic V/STOL fighter around a vectored-thrust engine with plenum chamber burning (PCB). There will inevitably be some penalties associated with V/STOL, since this seems likely to require additions to the basic engines (such as rotatable nozzles or separate lift engines) and a reaction control system for low speeds. Nevertheless, there is no reason to suppose that the overall penalty will be severe, provided the V/STOL aircraft is compared with a CTOL design of high thrust/weight ratio.

A Good Try But No Cigar

The argument so far has established that CTOL aircraft are very susceptible to the effects of runway bombing, that NATO faces a serious threat of airfield attacks in various forms, and that dispersal capability through the use of v/STOL aircraft is the only way to ensure survival. It is nonetheless admitted that v/STOL involves some penalty in terms of warload-radius performance, although it is arguable that the penalty would be slight in the case of an aircraft that needs a high thrust/weight ratio to meet its in-flight performance demands.

Accepting that some v/STOL penalty exists, it still seems logical to suppose that a significant number of overseas air forces would have adopted a v/STOL element for survivability. In reality, no such move has taken place. Some 20 years after the first flight of a production Harrier (on 31 August 1966), v/STOL has been adopted only by the RAF, RN, USMC, the Indian Navy, and the Spanish Navy, and only in relatively small numbers.

Considering first what might be termed the Harrier I generation, the RAF has bought a total of 124 single-seat GR.1/3s and 27 two-seat T.2/4s. These aircraft equip two operational squadrons in Germany (Nos 3 and 4 Sqn at RAF Gütersloh, each with 18 aircraft) and one in the UK (No 1 Sqn at Wittering), where the Operational Conversion Unit (No 233 OCU) is also located. The Wittering squadron can be deployed virtually anywhere in the world (as evidenced by past detachments to Belize and the Falklands), but in the event of a major war in Europe it would be used to reinforce either of NATO's flanks, i.e., Norway or Denmark in the north, or Italy, Greece or Turkey in the south. In the same circumstances, around 12 Harriers from the OCU would reinforce the Gütersloh wing in its forward deployment.

The USMC purchased from the British production line a total of 102 slightly modified Harrier GR.1s under the designation AV-8A (the remainder of which are now mostly converted to AV-8C standard) and eight two-seat TAV-8As. These aircraft initially equipped a training unit, VMAT-203, and two 'gun squadrons', VMA-231 and -542, at MCAS Cherry Point, North Carolina, and a third gun squadron, VMA-513 at MCAS Yuma, Arizona. However, the AV-8Cs are now in storage at Davis-Monthan AFB, Arizona, having been replaced by the McDonnell Douglas AV-8B, although the remaining TAV-8As temporarily soldier on.

The Spanish Navy bought 11 AV-8As (redesignated as the AV-8S Matador) and two TAV-8As. The transaction was carried out via the US Navy due to the Gibraltar problem, and the aircraft are currently operated as *Escuadrilla* 008. The unit is based at Rota, and has been routinely deployed in the carrier *Dédalo*.

The Sea Harrier differs in various respects from the Harrier GR.3, but in terms of a basic airframe-engine combination it is still a first generation aircraft. The RN has bought 57 Sea Harrier FRS.1s and four two-seat T.4Ns. The RN has three anti-submarine carriers (HMS *Invincible*, *Illustrious*, and *Ark Royal*), but there are only two operational Sea Harrier units, Nos 800 and 801 Sqn, although a third (No 809 Sqn) was formed temporarily during the Falklands conflict of 1982. The headquarters and training unit is No 899 Sqn, based at RNAS Yeovilton.

The Indian Navy has so far purchased a total of 23 Sea Harrier FRS.51s and four two-seat T.60s. These aircraft equip No 30 (White Tiger) Sqn, based at Goa in India, and will be deployed when necessary in the INS *Vikrant*. In the future Indian Sea Harriers will also operate from *Hermes*, which has been bought by India and is being renamed the INS *Virrat*.

Taking all five services together, these figures give a first generation total of 317 single-seaters and 45 two-seaters, providing a combined firm total of 362 members of the Harrier I series. The only serious prospect of increasing this number currently appears to be a possible Sea Harrier order from Italy, associated with the new carrier *Giuseppi Garibaldi*.

Turning to the second generation, the McDonnell Douglas AV-8B Harrier II, this has a far better warload-radius performance and in the long term should export in larger numbers, although its unit price appears to be higher than that for a Sea Harrier. The USMC plans to acquire 300 single-seaters and 28 two-seat TAV-8Bs. The RAF is to have a minimum of 94 AV-8Bs, which will be slightly modified and assembled in the UK by British Aerospace under the designation Harrier GR.5/7. In addition, the Spanish Navy is to purchase 12 AV-8Bs, presumably for operation from the new carrier *Principe de Asturias*.

The current totals for the second generation are thus 406 single-seat AV-8Bs and 28 TAV-8Bs, giving a combined total of 434 aircraft on current plans. As this book went to press in late 1988, No 1 (F) Sqn at Wittering had received 'a few' Harrier GR.5s and it is understood that No 3 (F) in RAF Germany would be the next to convert. It is also worth noting that in USMC service the AV-8B is replacing not only the AV-8A, but also the A-4M Skyhawk.

If the two Harrier generations are taken together, a combined production total of 764 aircraft planned to date is clearly not a catastrophic failure. On the other hand this figure may create a misleading impression of market penetration, simply because it includes large numbers of Harrier IIs that are replacing Harrier Is.

To put the figure of 764 Harriers into true perspective, it is necessary to consider how long it has taken to achieve that figure (which assumes USMC plans are fulfilled) and how few overseas operators have been convinced of the merits of V/STOL. The Hawker P.1127 first hovered in 1960 and completed transitions between jetborne and wingborne flight in the following year. In 1965 the Kestrel tripartite evaluation trials (by a combined UK/US/German unit) were conducted at West Raynham, and an initial order was placed for the P.1127 (RAF). This became the Harrier, which entered service in 1969, the AV-8A following in 1971. The first Sea Harrier had its maiden flight in 1978, and deliveries began in the following year. The first full-scale development AV-8B also flew in 1978, and VMA-331, the first of eight gun squadrons (replacing five A-4M and three AV-8C units) was declared operational in mid-1986.

It has thus taken more than a quarter-century from the time that the wheels of the first P.1127 left the ground for the production run to reach worthwhile numbers, and then only if two generations of aircraft are considered, including future projections. However, the grim reality of V/STOL marketing is more accurately conveyed by the fact that exports of the first generation amounted to only 150 aircraft to three operators, all of which were naval air arms, and that exports of the second generation so far amount to only 74 aircraft to two customers, both of which are existing V/STOL operators.

Thus, despite the unique operational advantages that V/STOL provides in avoiding the effects of airfield attacks, in naval use, and in world-wide deployments, and despite the excellent warload-radius performance of the second generation, the Harrier series has so far merely scratched at the surface of the global market. To put the figure of 150 exported first generation Harriers in perspective, when former chief test pilot A W (Bill) Bedford became sales manager for HSA Kingston in 1967, he said that he planned to repeat the success of the Hunter and sell 2,000 aircraft. At the time this appeared a perfectly reasonable target, bearing in mind the operational arguments in favour of V/STOL and the fact that the Harrier was the only V/STOL aircraft available. If one excludes the USMC sale (America being outside the sales department's terms of reference), the actual total achieved was a mere 32 aircraft, of which 13 were conditional on the US purchase!

In short, the Harrier I was a technological success, but a disaster in the marketplace. The manufacturer (HSA) quite clearly believed that at last it had a product that would win back much of the market share lost to the French. By HSA standards a large sales team was established and money was spent lavishly on marketing the aircraft overseas, but to no avail. Bill Bedford is one of the country's best aviation marketing men, and (having been chief test pilot throughout the early years of the project) he knows all about flying the Harrier. He also had some good salesmen working for him. Nonetheless, had it not been for Maj Gen Keith McCutcheon, then USMC Deputy Chief of Staff (Air), seeing a Harrier sales film (which Bedford's department was responsible for), then the marketing effort would have been a total flop.

For years those concerned with Harrier marketing tried to explain how it was that an aircraft that offered so much should be so difficult to sell. It was felt in the early days that operational studies could prove the value of the Harrier in terms of ordnance delivery rates, but potential customers seemed to have little faith in such analyses. More surprising was the fact that the Falklands conflict of 1982 brought no sales, despite the magnificent performance of both RN and RAF aircraft. If that conflict proved anything, it was probably the resistance of most air forces to any fundamental change in their concepts of operations.

In an effort to throw some light on this attractive yet (so far) largely unsaleable concept, the following chapters discuss the likely consequences for CTOL/STOL aircraft of attacks on NATO airfields, the other advantages of V/STOL (including the lessons of the Falklands conflict), and then the practical drawbacks and the other arguments that militated against the widespread adoption of such aircraft. Finally, the book outlines those advanced V/STOL programmes that are currently being funded, and discusses the direction that such developments should take in the future.

2 A Short History of Airfield Attacks

The case for the v/STOL combat aircraft is strongest in the naval context, due to its ability to use significantly less expensive operating platforms. However, the v/STOL aircraft will never make major inroads into the CTOL market until it is accepted by several of the principal air forces for land-based use. To this extent the future of the v/STOL aircraft depends on a new (and arguably more realistic) perception of the wartime threat to airfields.

Whereas a number of navies may buy v/STOL aircraft simply because they cannot afford conventional carriers, practical marketing experience indicates that no air force is going to buy v/STOL aircraft because it cannot afford to build conventional runways. In the end the concept will stand or fall according to whether the leading operators accept that their airfields may be seriously damaged or even destroyed in wartime, and that it is worth paying some price to ensure that they can continue to conduct operations despite any likely level of attack.

Counter-Air Operations

In considering the history of counter-air operations, it may be recalled that the first role for military aeroplanes was observation, or what we would now call tactical reconnaissance, effectively extending the horizon of the tethered balloon. The balloon had been in use for such duties in France since 1793, and continued to be employed to the end of WW1 in 1918. With the improvement in aerial cameras and the introduction of radio telegraphy, the aeroplane became a significant factor in determining the outcome of a land or naval battle, and consequently there was a demand for counter-air operations.

One way to achieve some degree of control of the air was aerial combat, which at the outset was aimed at ensuring that one's own side could carry out observation missions (essentially to provide warning of enemy troop concentrations prior to attacks), while the enemy was denied similar facilities. A more formal and modern definition of what is now termed 'air superiority' is (from USAF sources) 'that degree of dominance in the air battle of one force over another, which permits the conduct of operations by the former and its related land, sea and air forces at a given time and place without prohibitive interference by the opposing force'.

Returning to WW1, in the various governments' efforts to sustain popular support for a war involving horrific casualties for negligible results, combat between aircraft provided a welcome relief from the fighting in the trenches. Above all, it gave civilian populations the heroes they wanted. At last there were men who single-handedly produced quantifiable results in an environment that appeared to retain something of the honourable traditions of knightly combat. The fighter pilot was thus a gift for public relations, although his real contribution to winning the war probably bore no resemblance to his media image.

In winning control of the air, it was found that combat between the fighting scouts suffered a serious problem, in that the overall advantage had an unfortunate habit of swinging from one side to the other with each new technical development. Thus the 'Fokker Scourge', made possible by the introduction of a synchronized machine gun firing through the propeller of the Fokker E.1 monoplane, began on 15 June 1915, but in the course of 1916 the balance swung back in favour of the Allies.

This first reversal was brought about by the arrival of new and superior British and French aircraft with interrupter gear (the Sopwith $1\frac{1}{2}$ Strutter, Pup and Triplane, the Nieuport 17 and Spad 7). Conversely, by late 1916 the Germans had introduced the improved Halberstadt and Albatross D-series biplanes, and the balance swung back in their favour. In the summer of 1917 the Allies produced the Sopwith Camel, Bristol Fighter and Spad 13, each equipped with twin synchronized machine guns, and better aircraft than their German contemporaries. The balance swung only one more time, with the introduction in April 1918 of the Fokker D.VII biplane, the best fighter to see active service during that war.

Thus, although the qualities of the individual pilots were crucial when the opposing aircraft were evenly matched, it was clear that the results of the air battle tended to ebb and flow with the various phases of technical progress. Since each side wanted consistent results, the obvious lesson was to find some form of operation that provided the desired control of the air without relying on superiority in fighters, as measured in air combat.

The most realistic alternative to aerial combat was to attack enemy airfields, strafing aircraft on the ground and bombing their hangars, preferably in dusk or dawn raids. Air defences were still in their infancy, and a surprise strike out of a low sun often produced a much better kill-ratio than the dogfights so beloved by the press.

The Big One

Over 20 years later at the outbreak of WW2, operational aircraft were generally still using grass fields, but the rapid trend toward high tyre pressures (to make it possible to retract the mainwheels into a thin wing) brought a growing reliance on paved runways. It became standard practice to disperse aircraft in sandbagged revetments to reduce their susceptibility to bomb damage, but they were still suitable targets for strafing attacks, and their maintenance hangars could still be bombed.

In the German attack on Belgium, the Netherlands and northern France, beginning on 10 May 1940, some 3,000 combat aircraft were used to strike at 72 airfields. In one day alone approximately 500 aircraft were destroyed, mainly on the ground. On 22 June 1941 the *Luftwaffe* attacked two-thirds of the airfields in the four Russian border districts, and around 800 Soviet aircraft were destroyed on the ground (plus 400 in the air).

Air defences improved (particularly on the German side), but it was nonetheless possible for USAAF bomber formations to carry out medium/high level daylight carpet bombing that turned the whole area into a moonscape, and made several cuts in the runways. However, it was found that attacks had to be repeated frequently if a particular airfield was to be kept out of operation, since runways could be repaired in 12–18 hours. Today we still see photographs of WW2 airfields that were subjected to sustained bombing; they are often used in v/stol advertisements, although they have little relevance to modern attack techniques.

One of the most dramatic examples of airfield attack during WW2 occurred in the Low Countries early in the morning of 1 January 1945, when ten wings of German fighters strafed 27 Allied airbases. The attacking force consisted of approximately 650 FW 190s and 450 Me 109Ks, operating in three massive formations led by Ju 188s. They destroyed almost 300 aircraft on the ground, including 123 at Brussels/Evère alone.

Reports indicate that the Germans lost 57 of the attacking aircraft to British and American AAA, and 36 more to the Tempests and Spitfires that managed to get into the air. The *Luftwaffe* had pulled off a quick coup that virtually paralysed Allied tactical air power in that region for a week, and gave a favourable kill-ratio of approximately 3:1 at a time when air combat results were running strongly against the German side.

Surprise has been an important factor in many successful airfield attacks. The prime examples include the Japanese Navy's air attack on Hickham Field, a sideshow to the strike against Pearl Harbor that began at 7.55 am on Sunday 7 December 1941. Operating from a point 240 nm (445 km) north of the target area, Admiral Nagumo's carriers launched a total of 353 aircraft in two waves. The leading role in the attack on us warships was played by the Nakajima B5N2 *Kate* torpedo-bomber, but in airfield strikes the two principal types involved were the Aichi D3A1 *Val* bomber and the Mitsubishi A6M2 Zero fighter. Only 29 Japanese aircraft were lost, representing 8.2 per cent of the force. Balanced against this, they sank or damaged 18 us warships, destroyed 200 us aircraft, and killed or wounded 3,581 us military personnel.

Due to a six-hour time difference, it was not possible for Japanese aircraft to make a daylight strike against airfields on the Philippines before those on the ground had been made aware of the attack on Pearl Harbor. Nonetheless, nearly 100 us aircraft were destroyed around Manila (mainly on the ground) for the loss of only seven Japanese aircraft.

Middle East and Indo-Pakistan Conflicts

In more recent years the classic example of a surprise attack on airfields was the Israelis' pre-emptive onslaught against Arab bases during the Six-Day War of June 1967. Although quite recent, it involved what should logically have been obsolete attack methods, taking advantage (as the Japanese had done 25 years earlier) of the fact that war had not been declared. The Israelis flew a total of 3,279 sorties, attacked 28 airfields, and destroyed 391 aircraft on the ground (and 78 in flight).

According to reports that subsequently reached military circles, a typical Arab airfield was then defended by around 100 barrels of AAA, and 40 smaller automatic weapons. In spite of this, the Israelis were able to carry out 40-degree dive attacks along the runway centrelines, dropping sticks of 500 lb (227 kg) bombs that achieved a 70 per cent hit probability. Just as though they were attacking lightly-defended targets, each Israeli aircraft made a total of three or four passes, first bombing the runways then strafing aircraft and support facilities.

The Israeli loss rate in these attacks was approximately three per cent (i.e., three aircraft per 100 sorties flown), in line with the widely-accepted rule of thumb that the attacker must expect to lose at least one per cent on each pass. This ballpark figure has considerable statistical support from a variety of conflicts, and provides a sound argument for avoiding repeat attacks, unless the circumstances are exceptional. To illustrate the magnitude of the operation, on the first day of the Six-Day War the Israelis flew approximately 500 sorties and lost 15 aircraft, although the results achieved (in terms of a virtual cessation of Arab air effort) certainly justified such attrition.

It may be noted that after this conflict the Egyptians were advised by the Russians to line the AAA alongside the runways to minimize errors in lead-angle prediction. The Egyptians began using hardened aircraft shelters (HAS) of steel and concrete, covered in sand. The Israelis were already using such shelters, though of a different design. The Egyptians also began building airfields in the grassy areas of the Nile delta, where they were less readily detected by attacking pilots than in regions of barren desert.

The subsequent Yom Kippur War of October 1973 was likewise a surprise attack, but in this case it was the Arabs that were on the offensive, and there were no noteworthy strikes against Israeli airfields. However, on roughly the same time-scale there was a brief conflict between India and Pakistan, lasting from 3rd to 17th

The single runway of Port Stanley airfield, looking west, prior to the post-conflict extension. (*RN*)

December 1971, in which airfield attacks were to play a significant role. In particular, in East Pakistan (subsequently Bangladesh) around 16 Sabre 6s of No 14 Sqn were grounded within 24 hours of the start of hostilities due to runway damage caused by bombs dropped by Indian Air Force MiG-21s. The airfield was at Tejgaon, Dacca, and the bombs were released in pairs in shallow dives. Reports at the time indicated that these were rocket-accelerated 'dibber' bombs, but it seems more likely that they were conventional bombs with time-delay fuzes, giving separate craters at the impact point and where the charge was actually detonated below the paving. It may be noted that the Indian Air Force also employed large' numbers of small steel pyramids, that were dropped from auxiliary fuel tanks, and were coated with adhesive that effectively welded them to the runway target. There was one reported incident, in which a PAF Mirage blew a tyre while taxying, but on the whole this weapon system appears to have been ineffective.

The War in the South Atlantic

Other methods of airfield attack were used in the course of the Falklands/Malvinas conflict of 1982. The airport at Port Stanley on East Falkland was an attractive target for Britain, since it was one of the few that could be attacked without fear of civilian casualties. Aside from acting as a base for close support aircraft (IA-58 Pucará, Beech T-34C and Aermacchi MB.339), it was mainly being used as a logistics airhead for night-time C-130 flights from Argentina. These flights could not be intercepted by the Sea Harrier, due to that aircraft's inability to detect targets in a look-down mode over land, hence the only way to stop these reinforcements was to bomb the runway. There was also a possibility that Argentine Mirages, A-4s and Super Etendards might be operated from Port Stanley (then the only suitable paved runway on the islands), to give a quick reaction capability at some cost in warload and radius.

In the event the Argentines decided that, when wet, the airfield was unsuitable for all such high performance aircraft. At that time the runway was only 4,250 ft (1,300 m) long, although after the Argentine surrender it was extended by 2,000 ft (600 m) to take RAF C-130 Hercules and F-4 Phantoms. Arresters were added to deal with F-4 overruns. This was the practical limit for extension

at Port Stanley, and a larger airfield was subsequently constructed at Mount Pleasant at a cost of £276 million to accept reinforcement flights by RAF TriStars. This new base has an 8,500 ft (2,600 m) main runway, with a secondary strip of 5,000 ft (1,500 m). The air defence F-4s were moved to Mount Pleasant in May 1986.

The runway at Port Stanley was a very difficult target for British bombing attacks in 1982, since it was built directly on the natural rock, with hardcore filling the depressions. Any bomb crater would thus be smaller than normal, and easier to repair. From the defenders' viewpoint the runway was not only short (even the Pucarás were reported to be limited in take-off weight), but also the subject of a mud problem, since the local water table was very high. When the RAF took over, the runway was covered in AM-2 aluminium planking with a canvas underlay to keep the surface as dry as possible.

British forces attacked the runway in various ways. Three bombing runs were made by flight-refuelled Vulcans based on Ascension Island, each aircraft making a medium-level radar-bombing attack with 21 1,000 lb (454 kg) bombs. Being built on a distinctively-shaped peninsula, the airfield made a good target for such attacks, and it is probably fair to say that the RAF was unlucky not to have achieved better results.

The technique used was to approach low for the final 300 nm (550 km), flying at around 250 ft (75 m) and 340 knots (630 km/hr), then to pull up to 10,000 ft (3,000 m) for the bombing run. All 21 bombs were released in a single stick at around 30 degrees to the runway direction, a widely accepted procedure. The philosophy behind this approach appears to be that the use of a more acute angle risks the whole stick falling to one side of the runway, while a larger angle increases the cross-runway distance between craters, and may thus leave a usable width of paving.

On the first strike the first bomb is believed to have hit the runway centreline, while the next slightly damaged one edge of the runway, and the rest marched off across the field. The Argentines quickly repaired the main crater, although there are differing accounts of the smoothness of the resulting surface. The two subsequent sticks appear to have fallen slightly to the west of the runway, although the timing of release was better than in the first case.

An RAF Vulcan dropping a stick of up to 21 retarded 1,000 lb (454 kg) bombs. (*MOD*)

A Royal Navy Sea Harrier FRS.1 of No 809 Sqn, landing vertically on a carrier deck. Note the partially opened airbrake, to improve directional stability at low speeds. (HMS *Invincible*)

Stanley airfield was attacked many times by Sea Harriers and Harrier GR.3s, although they lacked the ability to damage the runway severely. Generally approaching at low level to minimize the risks associated with airfield defences, they tossed 1,000 lb (454 kg) bombs from a distance of around 3 nm (5.6 km) using a mixture of contact and airburst fuzes. The BL755 cluster bomb, weighing 600 lb (270 kg), was released in pop-up attacks at a height of 150–200 ft (45–60 m) against parked aircraft and the airfield hangars. Sea Harriers also used their radar to make blind level attacks against the airfield from offset IPs (initial points).

Although none of these attacks cratered the runway, there appears to have been some scabbing. The first officer to command RAF Stanley (Gp Capt King) remarked that he would have been very reluctant to operate fast jets from the runway's scabbed surface.

The case of Stanley airport has been considered in some detail because it illustrates several aspects of the modern airfield attack problem. Firstly, it demonstrates that in order to achieve the runway penetration (and hence the area of pavement upheaval) needed to cause an airbase to cease operations, conventional bombs have to be dropped from a significant height. They also have to be delivered very accurately, or in a long stick that allows for along-track aiming errors.

Unfortunately for the attacker, a relatively heavy bomber is needed to carry the number of bombs demanded to achieve this 'linear-shotgun' effect. Conversely, accurate dive-bombing with small warloads, as was employed by Israeli fighters in 1967, is a thing of the past in all but the most unsophisticated environments.

In the case of Stanley airfield, the defensive envelope was taken to have a radius of 20,000 ft (6,100 m), corresponding to the range of the Euromissile Roland SAM. The general aim in planning attacks was to remain above or beyond this radius. Sea Harriers bombed from above that height, and (together with GR.3s) tossed bombs in preplanned loft manoeuvres that kept the aircraft out of the reach of ground fire. They undoubtedly created some damage to the airfield, and may have 'agitated the Argies', but a maximum load of three bombs per aircraft gave little chance of cutting the runway with such attacks. The only way in which the RAF could reliably have hit the runway was to use laser-guided bombs (LGBs) and a designator in a two-seat Harrier, but no-one had forseen that such a requirement would arise.

On those occasions that the attacking aircraft went inside the defensive envelope of Stanley airfield, they flew at extremely low level, which ruled out the possibility of conventional bombs piercing the runway. To provide useful results against paved surfaces from such heights demanded special weapons that were not in the RAF inventory.

The attacks on Stanley airfield also illustrate the growing importance of defence-suppression in airfield attacks. The Vulcans from Ascension made two attacks with the Sperry/Texas Instruments AGM-45 Shrike anti-radar missile (ARM), the first strike damaging the main Westinghouse TPS-43F surveillance radar at Port Stanley (though this was operational again within 24 hours), and the second scoring a direct hit on an Argentine Army Contraves Skyguard radar on the airfield. Two missiles had been fired on each occasion.

A different form of defence suppression was illustrated by the first Sea Harrier attack on the airfield on 1 May 1982, following a few hours after the first Vulcan bombing run. In this case the attack was made by a total of nine aircraft, each of the first four tossing three 1,000 lb (454 kg) bombs at AAA/SAM sites, followed five seconds later by the second wave, which carried out the main attack. Four of these aircraft each carried three BL755 cluster weapons, which were used against parked aircraft, hangars, and targets of opportunity, while the fifth aircraft delivered retarded bombs against the runway. These retarded bombs may have added to the scabbing mentioned earlier, but they certainly did not produce sizeable craters.

Aside from demonstrating the need for special weapons to penetrate runways from low level delivery, and for defence suppression attacks against radars and AAA/SAM sites, the Falklands affair illustrated the substantial lengths of runway required by conventional aircraft, especially in terms of landing performance. It is also noteworthy that the V/STOL Sea Harriers, which were later to find the Stanley runway more than adequate, operated in the air defence role (i.e., at a useful, though not maximum, weight) from an 850 ft (260 m) strip of aluminium planking near the landing area at San Carlos, a strip only one-fifth the length of the runway that was too small for Mirages, A-4s and Super Etendards.

Before leaving the subject of the Falklands conflict, it may also be noted that, in order to avoid the effects of airfield attacks, some Pucarás were dispersed off the airfield to road sites that proved completely secure. This was not fully dispersed operation in the Harrier sense, as the Pucarás had to return to the airfield for refuelling and rearming, prior to flying their operational missions.

To summarize the airfield attack lessons of the Falklands, the conflict was a useful example of comparatively modern airfield demands and attack techniques, but from a weapons technology aspect it represented a transitional stage, before the RAF was able to use LGBs with an airborne designator, or special munitions that (despite low level delivery) would crater runways and discourage repairs.

Attacks in Africa

As it happened, the first use of modern runway attack weapons came in Chad in February 1986. France and Libya had been in conflict four times between 1968 and 1984, and on the last occasion the Libyan-backed rebels of Goukouni-Weddeye had been halted in their drive south only at the 16th Parallel, a situation that gave them control of almost half the country. On 14 September 1984 an agreement was signed between France and Libya under which they would simultaneously withdraw their forces, but this document was honoured only by France.

Libya's Colonel Gaddafi continued to pour men and materiel into the rebel-held north. To act as a logistics airhead for Libyan aircraft, an airfield was built at Ouadi-Doum. The runway is 12,500 ft (3,800 m) long and 200 ft (60 m) wide, flanked by taxyways to eliminate the clouds of sand that would otherwise be created by each take-off or landing. The airfield was used by all types of Libyan transport aircraft: the Ilyushin Il-76, Lockheed C-130 Hercules, Aeritalia G.222 and Fokker F.27-600.

Ouadi-Doum was also seen by Libya as a potential base for operational aircraft. Six Siai-Marchetti SF.260 light attack aircraft were positioned there, and were represented as the initial air arm of the rebel forces. More significantly, hardened shelters were built for a squadron of jet fighters, the implication being that Libyan Air Force combat aircraft (e.g., MiG-23s) would be based there as a counterbalance to any French *Armé de l'Air* Mirage F.1s and Jaguars that might be positioned at N'Djamena (the capital) to assist Chadian government forces.

On 14 February 1986 President Hissene Habre of Chad in conversation with French Defence Minister Paul Quilès requested air intervention against Ouadi-Doum under the terms of the 1976 defence agreement between the two countries. At that stage French air assets had been withdrawn from Chad to other ex-colonies in Africa. However, 12 Jaguars and six Mirage F.1s were quickly moved from Dakar in Senegal and Libreville in Gabon, to be based at Bangui M'Poko in Central Africa, together with one Boeing C-135F tanker. The crews of two *Aéronavale* Breguet Atlantic patrol aircraft, which were equipped with a comprehensive array of electronic sensors and based at Libreville (along with a second C-135F) were also briefed to support the mission. Reports indicate that a USAF E-3A AWACS aircraft flying over the Sudan monitored the operation, and that two Transall tankers were airborne during the mission as back-ups for the C-135Fs.

The strike took place on Sunday 16 February 1986 at 0800 hr local time, to make possible an attack out of a low sun, and to permit the first refuelling of the Jaguars to take place in daylight. Press reports gave a strike radius of 810 nm (1,500 km), although maps in some newspapers show Ouadi-Doum to be almost 1,000 nm (1,850 km) from Bangui.

The operation began at 0300 hr, when the two Atlantics took off from Libreville to guide the combat aircraft from Bangui to their refuelling points and to the target. They were also to monitor electronic transmissions in the area, and if necessary to direct rescue operations if any of the aircraft were shot down. At 0515 hr the first C-135F took off from Bangui, followed by the second from Libreville at 0530 hr.

At 0545 hr eight of the available Jaguars and four Mirage F.1s began to take off from Bangui. The Jaguars came from the 11th *Escadre de Chasse* (EC 11), which is normally based at Toul in France, while the Mirage F.1s were from the 5th *Escadre* (EC 5), which has its home base at Orange.

The standard *Armée de l'Air* airfield attack configuration for the Jaguar is 18 Thomson-Brandt BAP100 runway-piercing bombs on the centreline position, and two drop tanks on the inboard wing pylons. However, one report indicates that in this case each of six Jaguars had 24 BAP100s divided between the inboard pylons, and a single 265 Imp gal (1,200 litre) tank below the fuselage. On the outboard pylons each Jaguar carried a PHIMAT chaff/flare

French Air Force Jaguars carried out a series of successful attacks against Libyan air bases during the civil war in Chad. The Jaguar seen here is wearing the desert camouflage used for operations against Libyan and rebel targets during the conflict. (*Chuck Stewart*)

A Libyan Air Force Tupolev Tu-22 *Blinder* performed a classic high-level bombing run against the French-controlled N'Djamena airfield in Chad, dropping a stick of four 1,100 lb (500 kg) bombs on the main runway. This Iraqi Tu-22 is seen here escorted by an F-4J Phantom of the US Navy squadron VF-51 'Sundowners'. (*US Navy*)

dispenser pod and a Thomson-CSF Baracouda jamming pod. Each of the remaining two Jaguars carried four 800 lb (400 kg) retarded bombs in place of the BAP100s.

The outbound flight and the first refuelling took place at around 16,400 ft (5,000 m), despite considerable turbulence. At 240 nm (450 km) from the target the tankers turned back. At 0743 hr the Jaguars let down to avoid detection by the 125 nm (230 km) *Spoon Rest* surveillance radar and the 100 nm (185 km) *Flat Face* target acquisition radar at Ouadi-Doum. The aircraft cruised initially at 420 knots (780 km/hr), accelerating and dropping to 100 ft (30 m) as they approached the airfield.

Ouadi-Doum was protected by two SA-6 *Gainful* batteries with *Long Track* and *Straight Flush* radars (a third was installed subsequently), six ZSU-23-4 self-propelled quadruple-barrel 23 mm AAA units with *Gun Dish* radars, and at least one armoured vehicle with four SA-9 *Gaskin* missiles.

The Jaguars attacked in pairs with 30-second spacings, the first six aircraft with BAP100s and the last pair with the retarded HE bombs. Reports indicate that the BAP100s made six runway cuts, leaving a maximum ground roll of 2,625 ft (800 m). This was a short enough distance to prevent most combat aircraft from landing, though not so short as to prevent a high-powered aircraft taking off at reduced weight.

The attacking aircraft departed the target area at low level and 540 knots (1,000 km/hr), remaining low for a distance of around 100 nm (185 km), then climbed to 33,000 ft (10,000 m) to link up with two of the Mirage F.1s. At around 215 nm (400 km) south of the target these 10 aircraft met with the second C-135F, escorted by the two remaining Mirage F.1s, and the second series of refuellings began. At 1000 hr the first of the Jaguars touched down at Bangui; at 1030 the second C-135F landed at Libreville.

The Libyans, reportedly assisted by East German engineers, had the runway at Ouadi-Doum back in limited use on February 19th, i.e., three days after the attack, and it was fully operational by the 25th (nine days after the attack).

While the Libyans were repairing the effects of the Jaguar strike, France was preparing to protect N'Djamena against a retaliatory attack. Operation 'Epervier' (Sparrowhawk) involved the installation of an air defence system based on the Thomson-CSF R.440 Crotale low level SAM. However, before this system was

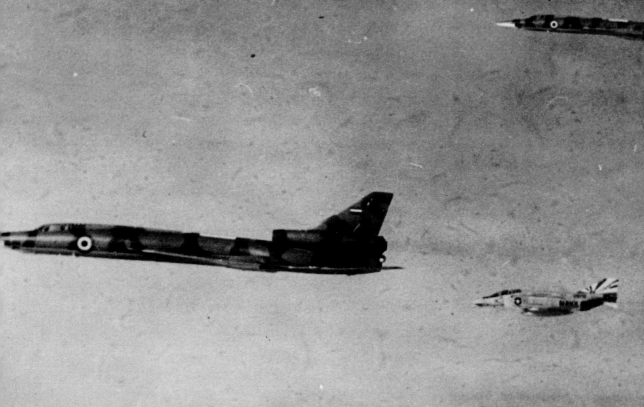

operational, a Libyan Air Force Tu-22 *Blinder* from Sabha airfield made a medium level strike against the main runway at N'Djamena on Monday the 17th (i.e., the day after the French attack).

The Tu-22 released a stick of four 1,100 lb (500 kg) bombs from a height of around 16,500 ft (5,000 m). The runway at N'Djamena is 9,185 ft (2,800 m) long and 130 ft (40 m) wide. In a remarkable example of runway bombing, the Tu-22 crew appears to have hit with all four, reducing the available length to 2,000 ft (600 m) for a period of 48 hours.

Reports state that the French then supplemented the Crotale, which has a ceiling of 11,800 ft (3,600 m), with the Raytheon Hawk SAM, which has a ceiling of 59,000 ft (18,000 m).

Raid on Libya

Following these strikes against the two respective airheads, the situation in Chad appears to have cooled somewhat, but in the next month there was a clash between Libya and the US in the Gulf of Sidra over the former's territorial limits. The background to this was that Libya claimed the area of sea below a line of Latitude 32 deg 30 min North, whereas the US recognized a territorial limit of only 12 nm (22.2 km) from the coast.

Early on 24 March 1986 ships of the US 6th Fleet entered the area claimed by Libya to exercise freedom of navigation in international waters. During the course of that day at least five SA-5 *Gammon* and one SA-2 *Guideline* missiles were fired at USN aircraft operating in support of these surface vessels. In retaliation, two Libyan patrol boats were attacked, and two Vought A-7E Corsair IIs fired Texas Instruments AGM-88A HARM (high-speed anti-radar missiles) at the SA-5 radar installation at Sirte. The attack was repeated in the early hours of the 25th. At that time the USN had the carriers *America*, *Coral Sea* and *Saratoga* in the region, though the last named was due to leave the Mediterranean shortly afterwards.

Tension between the two countries temporarily subsided, but on 5 April 1986 there was a Libyan-inspired terrorist attack on a nightclub in Berlin, as a result of which one US Army sergeant was killed and 230 other people were injured, including 50 US servicemen. In the light of growing evidence of a series of further terrorist attacks planned by Libya against US personnel and

Conventional carrier operations are illustrated by this US Navy Vought A-7E, about to be launched by a nosewheel-tow steam catapult. In the background a team of men prepare an F-14A for take-off. (*Tony Holmes*)

Existing CTOL naval attack aircraft are exemplified by this Grumman A-6E TRAM (target recognition attack multi-sensor). (*US Navy*)

installations, President Reagan decided to authorize a pre-emptive strike that would bring home to Col Gaddafi the cost of supporting terrorism.

Code-named *Operation El Dorado Canyon*, strikes were made against three targets around Tripoli and two near Benghazi at 0200 hr local time on Tuesday 15 April 1986. Successful attacks were made on two airfields: the military side of Tripoli airport, and Benina airbase near Benghazi.

The strikes were made by a combined force of USAF and USN aircraft, the former element operating from airfields in the UK. Since neither France nor Spain would permit overflights, the USAF strike radius was increased from around 1,300 nm (2,400 km) to approximately 2,500 nm (4,650 km). This gave a sortie duration of more than 12 hours, although the strike itself lasted only as many minutes. For tactical aircraft this was certainly a long mission, although it could not be compared with the Vulcan strikes from Ascension to the Falklands, at a radius of 3,256 nm (6,000 km).

Partly due to the long distances involved, the Libyan strike necessitated an unusually large ratio of supporting aircraft to those actually carrying out the bombing. In regard to tankers, the number positioned in the UK prior to the strike was built up to 32 KC-10 Extenders and 20 Boeing KC-135s, out of which a total of 28 (from RAF Fairford and RAF Mildenhall) actually took part in the operation. Electronic support was provided by five EF-111A Ravens (two of which were spares) from the 42nd Electronic Combat Squadron of the 20th Tactical Fighter Wing (TFW), based at RAF Upper Heyford, and by an unspecified number of Grumman EA-6B Prowlers from the two carriers, these aircraft reportedly giving jamming in both target areas. Radar surveillance over the region was provided by Grumman E-2C Hawkeyes, with combat air patrols (CAPs) flown by Grumman F-14A Tomcats, likewise from the carriers. Defence suppression was the mission of six F/A-18A Hornets from the USS *Coral Sea* and six Grumman A-6E Intruders from the USS *America*, using the 10 nm (18.5 km) AGM-45 Shrike and the 25 nm (46 km) AGM-88A HARM, a total of 30 HARMS and 12 Shrikes being fired at the various Libyan radars. Post-strike reconnaissance missions were flown by two Lockheed SR-71As from RAF Mildenhall.

The USAF strike force consisted of 24 General Dynamics F-111Fs from RAF Lakenheath, but six of these were spares that turned

A Grumman A-6E Intruder TRAM Intruder lands on the flight deck of the aircraft carrier USS *Coral Sea* (CV-43) during operations off the coast of Libya. (*US Navy*)

Thanks to one air-to-air refuelling en route and two on the return leg of the mission, 13 US Air Force F-111s from RAF Lakenheath in Suffolk, England, made precision attacks against targets in the Benghazi area of Libya during *Operation El Dorado Canyon*. (*Jon Davison*)

back after the first refuelling. Of the remaining 18, five aborted due to system failures or inability to find their specific targets, and 13 bombed. The USN strike force consisted of six A-6Es from the USS *America* and eight from the USS *Coral Sea*, but two aborted and 12 bombed the two targets in the Benghazi area. In all, around 100 aircraft were involved in the mission, out of which 32 carried out the main attacks, though only 25 of these actually bombed. There were four refuellings en route to the target, partly because some phases were flown at low level, and two refuellings on the return.

Although the Libyan Arab Air Defence Command (LAADC) fired a large number of SA-2 *Guidelines*, SA-3 *Goas*, SA-6 *Gainfuls* and SA-8 *Geckos*, most of these launches reportedly occurred after the strike had been completed. Both the F-111Fs and the A-6Es are believed to have made their attacks at around 500 knots (925 km/hr) and a height of 400 ft (120 m). In essence both types identified their target locations at long range on radar (the Texas Instruments APQ-119 in the F-111F, and the Norden APQ-148 in the A-6E) and then found their exact aiming points using forward-looking infra-red (FLIR) equipment (the Ford Aerospace AVQ-26 Pave Tack and Hughes Aircraft AAS-33 TRAM [Target Recognition/Attack Multisensor] respectively).

Pave Tack became operational with the 48th TFW in September 1981, and may be regarded as a day/night adverse weather derivative of the TV-based daylight Pave Knife system used successfully in Vietnam. Using FLIR, Pave Tack allows the operator to hold an aiming mark on a target, and to fire a co-axial laser that provides accurate slant-range, altitude and relative velocity for unguided bombs, and designation for LGBs. Some of the F-111Fs were armed with four 2,000 lb (910 kg) Texas Instruments GBU-10 Paveway 2 LGBs, while others each had 12 Mk 82 Mod 1 Snakeye 500 lb (227 kg) retarded bombs.

The TRAM system of the A-6E appears to function like Pave Knife, but without the laser designation facility. The Navy aircraft were armed with Mk 82 Snakeyes and the 490 lb (222 kg) Rockeye cluster bomb unit (CBU).

One of the useful features of Pave Tack (and possibly also of TRAM) is that a video recording of the IR picture assists in damage assessment. Aside from the strikes on the other three targets, it is estimated that between three and five Il-76s were destroyed at Tripoli airport, together with at least four MiG-23s, two Fokker

F.27s and two Mi-8 *Hip* helicopters at Benina. Hangars employed for MiG-23 maintenance were seriously damaged.

These strikes against the airfields at Tripoli and Benina were technically interesting, in illustrating the fact that precision low level night-time attacks are now possible, using a combination of radar, IR, and laser ranging and marking. However, on this occasion the object was to cause expensive damage, not to stop operations at the airfields.

One aircraft (an F-111F) was lost, reportedly due to AAA, although it may have been a pilot disorientation problem, and the crew of two were killed. One Arab newspaper report stated that the wreckage had been recovered from the Mediterranean and flown to Russia for examination. Another F-111F was forced to land at Rota in Spain due to an engine overheating problem, but recovered to the UK the following day.

Summary

The various airfield attacks mentioned in the forgoing discussion illustrated the use of a number of special weapons and techniques. The case of WW2 included many different forms of airfield attack, from strafing to carpet-bombing. Israel's Six-Day War demonstrated the value of precision dive-bombing along the runway centreline, although this relied on surprise and ineffective defences. It reportedly included the first operational use of 'dibber' bombs; the Israeli Military Industries' Condib-70.

The Falklands/Malvinas conflict included some vain attempts at medium level runway bombing, and some runway-scabbing from low level attacks with outdated weapons. Cluster weapons were used in forward-toss attacks against aircraft and airfield facilities from outside the range of airfield defences. The French attack on Ouadi-Doum in 1986 represented the first use of modern runway attack weapons, Thomson-Brandt BAP100s, in generating cross-runway cuts from low level release. The resulting medium-level attack on N'Djamena succeeded only because the airfield had only low level defences, and the bombing crew a great deal of luck. The US attack on the two Libyan airfields demonstrated that precision low level attacks can now be carried out at night, using special sensors. From a technology demonstration viewpoint, it is regrettable that the USAF aircraft did not take this opportunity to test the Matra Durandal runway-attack weapon.

3

The Threat to NATO Airfields

The Modern Airfield As A Target

As outlined in the first chapter, the role of tactical airpower has
changed considerably over the years, and control of the air is now
a vitally important factor in determining the outcome of the
ground battle. Indeed, for NATO forces on the Central Front the
unrestricted use of tactical airpower may well be the only way to
offset the general Warsaw Pact superiority in numbers.

Control of the air may be won either through combat between
fighters or by denying an opponent the use of his airbases. The kill-
ratio for aerial combat in a future conflict is impossible to predict,
since planners cannot assess with certainty the quality of enemy
aircraft and pilots. In contrast, heavy and sustained attacks on
airfields can undoubtedly produce significant results. Such attacks
will at least reduce the sortie rates achieved from these bases, and
they may pin down aircraft on the ground or force the dispersal of
CTOL (and even STOL) aircraft to secondary airfields. An unplanned
dispersal implies not only reduced facilities for rearming,
maintenance and repair, but also less effective air defences and
probably no aircraft shelters. The destruction of aircraft on the
ground will then be comparatively easy.

Operations from a military airfield may be interrupted in a
number of ways, though in recent years considerable efforts have
been applied to protecting the more vulnerable components.
Thus, whereas the 48–72 combat aircraft based at a typical fighter

airfield may in the past have represented high-value soft targets (though there would also have been some worthless decoys), aircraft are now generally protected in shelters that can be damaged seriously only by a direct hit. In consequence, an aircraft on the ground can now be put out of action only by a precision-guided munition (PGM). Further complicating the problem, not all the shelters will be occupied at any one time, hence some PGMs will inevitably be wasted. It may be added that the taxyways leading to the HAS are also useful targets, but they likewise require PGMs.

By the same token, fuel dumps and munition stores are now generally dispersed and camouflaged. In wartime, maintenance facilities would also be dispersed to some extent, although the destruction of hangars would cause some disruption of operations. Command, control and communications (c^3) facilities may likewise be hardened and dispersed, with backups provided to safeguard against their possible destruction by sabotage or other means.

Several items crucial to the smooth running of a military airfield may remain potential targets for special forces units on the ground, but the only positive high-value target for air attack now appears to be the runway itself. Although a difficult target in comparison with (for example) a taxying aircraft or a fuel bowser, the runway may be cut temporarily by a series of direct hits from a special runway attack system. Unlike every other essential component of the operation, the runway cannot be broken down into small parts and hidden in the surrounding countryside, or even camouflaged with any great success. The all-important runway is a fixed target of known location that is easily seen from a considerable distance, and—if suitably cratered—will inhibit or preclude further operations for a significant period of time.

A typical fighter runway is approximately 8,000 ft (2,450 m) long and 150 ft (45 m) wide, generally with an equally long taxy-strip of around half this width. A military runway surface (i.e., the concrete paving) in normally 10–12 inches (25–30 cm) thick in the case of a fighter base, although Soviet runways in the Arctic are almost 16 inches (40 cm) thick, and US bomber bases may have 24 inch (60 cm) paving.

Soviet tactical airfields are unusually difficult to put out of operation, because their runways are wider than those of their NATO counterparts, and because they have on either side of the runway an area of ground with a specially improved bearing capacity, allowing fighters to fly from the grass in emergency. Peacetime exercises have demonstrated that this off-runway operation really works, even when the airfield has experienced heavy rain, although it seems likely that the latest Soviet designs are less suitable for grass operation than their forebears.

It may be that the Warsaw Pact produces these special runway borders simply by improving drainage over the relevant area, but it is also possible that they are using pierced steel plate (PSP), or have added something to the soil to improve its bearing strength. During WW2 the Germans carried out extensive testing of methods to improve grass airfields, including ploughing cement into the top layer of soil. Far higher tyre pressures are now in general use, but there is also a much wider choice of aggregate materials available to strengthen the soil.

Before leaving the subject of Warsaw Pact air operations, it may be noted that the Pentagon document 'Soviet Military Power: 1986' attributes to the Pact forces a 'significant advantage over those of NATO in the degree of hardening completed at their tactical airbases. They have built several thousand concrete aircraft shelters, many of which are earth-covered for added protection and camouflage. The Soviets have established secondary operating strips for a number of their forward-based units, although they still have some space limitations for potential later reinforcements. . .'

To provide some indication of the difficulties involved in operating from grass, it is generally agreed that the maximum acceptable tyre pressure in the case of wet boggy grass is 30–45 psi (2.1–3.2 kg/cm^2), which is only a fraction of the pressures used by modern combat aircraft. The V/STOL Harrier has a nominal tyre pressure of 120 psi (8.5 kg/cm^2) and has operated from grass on many occasions, but in wartime would use paved surfaces to make its operations independent of weather. Soviet fighters of the MiG-21/Su-7 generation have pressures in the range 120–192 psi (8.5–13.5 kg/cm^2), which is somewhat low by modern standards. The F-15A and F-16A have pressures of 260 and 275 psi respectively (18.3 and 19.4 kg/cm^2), while naval aircraft such as the A-4 and F-4B have tyre pressures in the region of 370 psi (26 kg/cm^2).

In the case of NATO air operations, there is in general no off-

The General Dynamics F-16 can get off the ground in 1,000 ft (300 m), but needs a runway of roughly 5,000 ft (1,500 m) to ensure a safe recovery. (*GD*)

runway capability to be considered (although some aircraft may be dispersed to motorways), hence the airfield represents a fundamentally softer target than in the Warsaw Pact context. Disregarding for the moment the use of NBC and other area-denial weapons, the attacker's objective is to make a series of carefully-located cuts across the runway and taxyway, and across any long straight stretches of access way.

To give some feel for the magnitude of the bombing effort involved, it might be taken as a first approximation that the minimum take-off run for a conventional aircraft is 1,300 ft (400 m). Using the typical runway dimensions suggested previously, this criterion would imply the need for five equally-spaced cuts across the paving, or a total of 10 cuts if the taxyway is considered suitable for operations. However, access-ways would increase the number of cuts required.

One report on airbase survivability ('*Technology Solutions to the Runway-Denial Problem*' by John M Myres of the Flight Dynamics

Laboratory, Wright-Patterson AFB) suggested 16 cuts for a maximum residual run of 1,500 ft (460 m). This study was based on a typical NATO airfield layout, with aimpoints selected wherever possible to coincide with the choke-point intersections of runways and access-ways, and for collateral damage effects. The result would be 31 segments of residual surface, of which all but two would be less than 1,375 ft (420 m).

The end product of the attack would remain satisfactory as an operating base only for a member of the V/STOL Harrier family. No conventional aircraft could carry out ground attack missions from such short runs, although a modern fighter such as the F-16 could still take off in air defence configuration. This requires a ground roll of 1,100 ft (335 m) at 59°F (15°C), but the ground roll of the F-16 on landing is around 2,800 ft (850 m), which has to be factored up to perhaps 4,900 ft (1,500 m) to allow for the scatter of touchdown points. From the Warsaw Pact viewpoint an airfield attack that forces a wing of F-16s to take off at light weight (with a limited mission capability) and then land at an airfield where there are no shelters available would be at least a partial success. In ground attack terms the F-16s have lost an entire mission out of a short war, their c^3 problems have been magnified, and they are quite possibly left sitting out in the open, waiting to be strafed.

The late Sir Sydney Camm, chief designer of Hawker Aircraft, once said that a V/STOL combat aircraft would not amount to very much unless it had a performance in the category of the F-4 Phantom. This Phantom FG.1 from No 700 'Omega' Sqn, Royal Navy, is seen being catapulted from the deck of the aircraft carrier HMS *Ark Royal* in 1977. (*RN*)

Diverted Tornadoes (to consider another NATO case) may be separated from their special JP233/MW-1 munitions.

Before proceeding with this discussion of the effort needed to close NATO airbases, it is relevant to consider how quickly runway cuts can be repaired, and how much runway is actually needed by the various categories of aircraft involved on the NATO side.

Crater Repairs

The repair of a single bomb crater may provide sufficient runway width for an aircraft to take off, but several craters may have to be dealt with so that aircraft can land safely and so that a useful force can be put into the air in a short time. In addition, other craters may have to be filled so that aircraft can gain access from their shelters to the longest stretches of residual runway. The defenders might thus have to repair five or six holes before the worst effects of the bombing are eliminated. The clearance of area-denial minelets will be a further impediment to restarting operations.

It is questionable how many NATO airfields are normally equipped with the special vehicles and civil engineering equipment needed to deal with bomb craters. Without these provisions, the airfield would probably be out of action for the duration of a conventional war in Central Europe. Given the men and equipment, it has traditionally been estimated that each bomb crater takes four hours to repair. As a rule-of-thumb, a well-executed multi-cut attack could well (on this basis) close the airfield operationally for an entire day, eliminating two or three missions, corresponding to 100–200 sorties.

Since airfield denial attacks can be so effective, a great deal of effort in recent years has been directed at rapid runway repairs. The USAF Disaster Preparedness Regulation (ARF 93–2) describes a procedure by which three 750 lb (340 kg) bomb craters may be repaired by a team of 40 men in a period of four hours.

Prior to the late 1960s the task of repairing British airfields fell to the RAF Regiment, but since then it has been the responsibility of the British Army's Royal Engineers (RES). In Germany the four RAF airfields would be repaired by RE Construction Squadrons, reinforced by men from the TA (Territorial Army) and operating under the command of 39 Engineer Regiment. *The Statement on the Defence Estimates 1986* announced the intention to establish two more TA Airfield Damage Repair (ADR) Squadrons, making eight in

Matra Durandal explodes under a runway paving. (*Matra*)

all, to keep key RAF airfields in the UK operational. Each squadron is understood to consist of 180 men, with special vehicles, steel matting, and piles of hardcore prepositioned at the unit's airfield. In war each bomb crater would be filled with hardcore, which would then be compacted, and covered with quick-setting cement. Finally, a steel mat would be laid over it. According to press reports, a trained team will be able to carry out this temporary repair within two hours. In the case of RAF Germany at least this 'sticking plaster' repair is clearly adequate, since all four bases are expected to be overrun within a matter of hours.

Regarding the effect of area-denial minelets, anything on the surface would be swept away by an armoured bulldozer, but any charge lying below the surface could present problems. It nonetheless appears reasonable to suppose that the Soviet Union has followed the West in the development of submunitions that may be dispensed in large numbers over an airfield to pose a threat to aircraft, repair vehicles and personnel, and that some will be detonated with variable timing delays to discourage mine-clearing operations. It is thus difficult to estimate with confidence the time likely to be taken to repair the effects of bombing attacks against operating surfaces.

Allowing for rapid repair techniques and the delaying effects of randomly-scattered minelets, it might nonetheless be assumed that each crater will take at least two hours to repair, and that a heavy attack on the airfield will stop operations for something in excess of 12 hours. For comparison, during WW2 a heavily-attacked airfield was typically closed for 12–18 hours. If the attack is made at dawn, then a NATO airbase would be closed for one day out of a conventional war that is expected to last only five days. A forward base, such as Gutersloh, which is only 65 nm (120 km) from East Germany, may well be overrun within 12 hours of the start of hostilities. A single air attack might thus rule out its use for the duration. In any event, the restricted duration of the use of conventional weapons means that airfield attacks could have disproportionately serious effects. One day will be a long time in WW3.

How Much Runway Is Really Needed?

Having given some indication of the number of cuts required for one particular value of residual runway length, and discussed how quickly cuts may be repaired, the main question is how much concrete will a typical combat aircraft of the 1990s really need to continue operations.

Providing a practical answer to that question is complicated by several considerations. For example, there are large differences between the airfield performances of the various NATO types, and for any given type the take-off and landing demands will vary considerably with aircraft weight and to a lesser extent with ambient temperature, airfield altitude, slope and wind, and according to whether there is water on the runway.

A military runway is much longer and wider than is normally required for a single aircraft to take off and land. The margins provided allow for accelerate-and-stop distances in aborted take-offs, the greater widths required by formation take-offs, and the ability to continue operations despite some degree of damage or obstruction (for instance, due to peacetime repairs). Runway length also allows for a wide variation in touchdown points, which may be necessary with inexperienced pilots and in bad visibility.

Take-off ground-roll is computed as the distance required to accelerate to unstick speed. Acceleration depends basically on the aircraft's thrust/weight ratio, although at high weights drag becomes an important factor due to the associated unstick speeds. The speed at which the aircraft leaves the ground is a function of its wing loading (i.e., the ratio of weight to wing area) and the lift coefficient that is generated at unstick. This is normally far less than the maximum that the aircraft can attain, in order to avoid excessive drag in the climb-out.

Provided that the tailplane (or horizontal stabilizer) is sufficiently powerful to raise the nosewheel at the minimum theoretical unstick speed, then a high-powered aircraft may benefit from the vertical component of thrust produced by aircraft rotation, effectively reducing wing loading. In some aircraft (e.g., the Sepecat Jaguar) this effect is enhanced by the engines being installed at a positive angle to the longitudinal axis. Combining the effects of aircraft rotation and engine incidence, it may thus be possible to arrange for the thrust line to be at 15°–20° to the horizontal at unstick. If the aircraft has a thrust/weight ratio of unity (T/W = 1.0), then wing loading is in effect lessened by 25 to 35 per cent, reducing take-off ground roll by the order of 15 to 20 per cent.

As noted above, take-off distance varies with airfield altitude and ambient temperature, although this is naturally of little significance in Central Europe, compared to operations in (for instance) the Middle East. Hot, high take-offs reduce the thrust available for acceleration and simultaneously increase the speed

The Sepecat Jaguar is claimed to have a limited off-runway capability. (*BAe*)

at which the aircraft will unstick. Airfield performance is traditionally quoted for a flat, dry runway at sea level, with zero wind and an ambient temperature of 59°F (15°C). A summer ambient of 86°F (30°C) may easily increase take-off distance by the order of 15 per cent, relative to this standard value.

As a first approximation, the take-off distance for a given aircraft type varies with the square of the weight. A 20 per cent increase in take-off weight may thus be expected to produce almost a 45 per cent increase in ground roll and in the distance taken to clear the standard 50 ft (15 m) obstacle.

If typical examples of modern combat aircraft are considered, it is clear that maximum take-off weight may be 50 per cent heavier than clean weight with full internal fuel, hence the runway requirement may vary by a factor in excess of 2.0. If an 'escape' scenario is envisaged, in which the aim is simply to leave a bombed airfield with a view to continuing operations elsewhere, then the overall variation in ground run will be even greater, with the distance required for an escape at light weight equal to something in the region of only one third of that required for a take-off at maximum weight.

The take-off ground-roll criteria will clearly depend on the timescale for the study, and at any given time there will be a range of criteria to allow for the different types of aircraft in service. For simplicity, the following discussion is based on a single aircraft type attempting to operate from the target airfield. To impose the most difficult demands on the attacker, this resident aircraft is taken to be a fighter typical of the Eurofighter/Rafale/ATF generation.

In deciding how much effort is required to prevent this generic aircraft taking off, the attacker may well consider the following criteria:

(a) *an escape mission*, in which the aircraft is given around 50 per cent internal fuel, with a view to transiting to a nearby operating base. The minimum ground roll would then be approximately 1,000 ft (300 m), though it would be up to twice this length for an older aircraft such as the Jaguar.

(b) *an air defence sortie* with full internal fuel and four air-air missiles. The minimum acceptable ground roll would then be increased to the region of 1,300 ft (400 m).

(c) *a ground attack sortie* with full internal fuel and a heavy external load. Take-off roll would then be around 2,600 ft (800 m).

For comparison, the AV-8B can escape or fly an air defence sortie from vto, and its maximum take-off run is around 1,300 ft (400 m). It must also be emphasized that some form of safety factor would be applied to the computed ground roll for any aircraft, if only to allow for such variables as engine acceleration time.

To simplify the decision-making process, the attacker might well reduce the options to the 'escape' and ground attack cases. To prevent the aircraft on the ground from escaping, he would have to bomb the paved surfaces very intensively, so that there is no run of 1,000 ft (300 m) remaining. At the opposite extreme, to stop the airfield being used as a base for effective ground attack missions, the maximum residual ground run (ignoring for the moment where the aircraft is to land) should be less than approximately 2,600 ft (800 m). As we shall see later, there is a disproportionately large difference between the attack efforts required to achieve these two results.

Landing Performance

The attacker might alternatively take the view (bearing in mind all the other calls on his air-ground assets) that it is sufficient to prevent an aircraft landing back at its base. If he can force returning aircraft to divert to other bases, then all kinds of resources at these secondary airfields will be overloaded. Aside from the fact that sortie rate will be decreased, it is quite possible that these diverted aircraft will have to be parked in the open, where they may relatively easily be put out of action for the duration of hostilities.

Supporting this line of reasoning, it is generally the case that modern combat aircraft require more runway for landing than for take-off. The historical trend toward high thrust/weight ratios has kept take-off distances within check (despite high wing loadings), but has not helped landing performance, since in the ctol case engine thrust cannot be used to reduce touchdown speed or improve deceleration on the ground.

Conventional landing performance is basically a function of aircraft stall speed in the landing configuration, this speed being governed by wing loading and maximum lift coefficient. An aircraft with a stall speed of 100 knots (185 km/hr) has a ground roll of around 2,000 ft (600 m) under standard conditions, and takes perhaps 1,200 ft (370 m) to descend from a nominal 50 ft (15 m) obstacle height. These distances vary approximately with the square of the stall speed. The safe field length required for that particular case would be in the region of 3,700 ft (1,130 m), allowing for variations in touchdown point, water on the runway, etc. To put this figure in perspective, an F-4E reportedly has a minimum field length of 5,000 ft (1,525 m), and this is almost certainly dictated by landing performance.

Aside from minimising touchdown speed (which is a function of stall speed), the designer can reduce the safe landing distance in various ways. Thrust reversal or a braking parachute will reduce ground roll by perhaps a half or a third respectively. Using thrust reversal, a Tornado or Viggen can be brought to rest in as little as 1,300 ft (400 m).

The Saab Viggen family is probably the most survivable of CTOL combat aircraft. (*Saab*)

The Republic F-105 Thunderchief nuclear strike fighter was conceived at a time when enemy interdiction against American airfields was unthinkable. Hence, the miles of concrete required to operate a wing of Thunderchiefs were considered to be invulnerable. This example is the first production F-105B. (*Republic*)

The air distance can be halved by the use of a naval-type approach, eliminating the conventional round-out, although this demands an unusually strong undercarriage. The scatter of touchdown points can be reduced by some form of precision approach aid, though if this is ground-based it has to be highly mobile. The F-15 STOL demonstrator is to use its Hughes APG-70 high resolution radar for this purpose, and it is hoped to reduce touchdown scatter from $\pm$ 500 ft (150 m) to $\pm$ 60 ft (18.5 m).

In the context of reduced landing requirements, it is instructive to consider the claims made by Saab-Scania for the Viggen. According to the brochure, if the Viggen is operated conventionally, its landing roll is 3,000 ft (900 m) and the safe landing distance is 5,000 ft (1,500 m). Thrust-reverser cuts the ground roll to 1,300 ft (400 m), but the safety margin is unchanged, giving a demand of 3,300 ft (1,000 m). Auto-throttle to stabilize the approach speed cuts the scatter of touchdown points, as does the zero-flare short-landing technique. The final result is that the safety margin can be reduced to 330 ft (100 m).

In principle, the Viggen is thus capable of landing on a residual stretch of highway only 1,630 ft (500 m) long, according to the manufacturer's calculations. Nonetheless, in practice the Swedish Air Force (SAF) dispersal scheme would make use of substantially longer stretches of highway, the principal 'runway' at each site being 4,000–6,500 ft (1,200–2,000 m) long. Such lengths permit

Perhaps surprisingly, Sweden's new JAS 39 Gripen does not have thrust reversal, relying instead on a slow stall speed for short landing performance. (*JAS-IG*)

older aircraft such as the Draken to operate, and they also provide for some degree of damage to the paving, although the SAF does not appear to have published its own estimate for the minimum run suitable for Viggen operations.

The SAF concept of operations has the attraction that the dispersal sites are difficult to locate, and can be supplied economically by road. In addition, since these sites are positioned in wooded areas, the cost of hardened shelters can be avoided. Bunkers are provided for the men controlling the operation, but the servicing positions are simply camouflaged against enemy reconnaissance efforts.

In recent years the SAF dispersal concept has been modified, the resulting 'Air Base 90' plan being aimed at reducing the service's vulnerability to modern attacks on its operating sites. At the time that dispersal was first planned, ground attack aircraft typically carried small loads of simple HE bombs. Since it was difficult for the enemy to locate either the sites in use or the aircraft on the ground, the threat amounted to inaccurately delivered ineffective ordnance. Today all the operating sites are probably known to a potential enemy through satellite reconnaissance, and aiming errors can be compensated by the use of cluster weapons. In addition, a single aircraft using lightweight bombs can put one of the small 'runways' out of action, and it is probably impractical to equip every dispersed site for paving repairs. Under the new plan, short auxiliary runways of 2,600 ft (800 m) have been constructed, linked to the main roadway so that a series of operating surfaces are available.

These improved dispersed sites will presumably also be employed by the forthcoming JAS 39 *Gripen* (Griffon), which is required to be capable of operating from stretches of highway only 3,300 ft (1,000 m) long. Unlike the Viggen, the Gripen will have no thrust reverser (to save on unit cost), but it may be expected to retain all the Viggen's devices for reducing touchdown scatter, and the latter's zero-flare short landing technique. The Gripen will presumably have a slower stall speed than its predecessor.

Even if the basic landing performance of the aircraft is known precisely, it is still impossible to predict with confidence the safety margins that individual air forces would adopt in wartime. In the case of the lightly-loaded canard configuration fighters of the

Although not a STOL aeroplane, the Saab Draken (this is a J35F) would in emergency be operated from road sites. (*Saab-Scania, H-O Arpfors*)

1990s, with braking parachutes or thrust reversers, the ground roll may be as short as 1,300 ft (400 m). A landing roll of 1,000 ft (300 m) has been reported for the Rafale, but it is difficult to see how this could be achieved without arrester gear, which lacks the mobility required for operation from bombed runways.

To digress, there have been various attempts to develop land-based arrester systems, but they have achieved little acceptance beyond the prevention of occasional overruns. It is nonetheless worth noting that in early 1986 the first of a batch of 16 mobile arresting systems produced by Wickes Companies Inc for the USAF was delivered to Ramstein AB in West Germany. This system uses a pair of B-52 brake units, can reportedly be installed in 40 minutes, and can bring an aircraft of F-15 size to rest within 1,000 ft (300 m). It can arrest aircraft at up to 17 engagements per hour. The initial batch was purchased under a $3.9 million contract, and USAF plans call for the acquisition of a total of 128 of these systems by the end of FY88.

It may also be noted that the aim of the F-15 STOL demonstrator is to be able to operate from a residual runway length of 1,500 ft (460 m). However, this is only a target figure, and it does not appear to be a requirement for the ATF competitors. This writer would suggest that the minimum safe landing distance for the next fighter generation will be around 2,600 ft (800 m), although in the light of claims made by Dassault-Breguet and Saab-Scania, consideration should perhaps also be given to an absolute minimum distance of 2,000 ft (600 m).

Combining take-off and landing considerations, there appear to be several possible criteria for runway-cutting attacks on NATO airfields on the timescale of the next generation of fighters:

(a) to prevent the escape of these aircraft to an alternative operating base would require bombing to produce a maximum residual run of approximately 1,000 ft (300 m).
(b) to prevent these aircraft making ground attack sorties, the residual run should be no more than 2,600 ft (800 m).
(c) to make the runway unsuitable for landings, the maximum available run should be no more than 2,600 ft (800 m), although on some manufacturers claims 2,000 ft (600 m) will suffice.

Relating these bombing criteria to a typical 8,000 ft (2,450 m) NATO airbase, it is clear that the attacker may apply completely different levels of effort to achieve these various aims. At the one extreme, two well-placed cuts in the runway and two in the taxyway will produce residual runs of approximately 2,600 ft (800 m). At the other extreme, by extrapolating from the 16-cut USAF study mentioned earlier, it seems reasonable to assume that something in the region of 25 cuts would be required to give a maximum residual run of 1,000 ft (300 m).

In other words, the resident aircraft could probably be prevented from landing, and from taking off with worthwhile ground attack loads simply by making four cuts, whereas they could be prevented from escaping at light weight only by a major effort producing around 25 cuts. When allowances are made for attrition and supporting aircraft (mainly electronic warfare and defence suppression), the landing and ground attack criterion may represent around 12–15 sorties, and the escape criterion perhaps 50–60 sorties. In either case the attacker would presumably assess the damage soon after the strike and launch a small-scale supplementary strike to make good any missing cuts. However, this would not change the overall conclusion that the criteria extremes represent roughly a 4:1 ratio in sortie effort.

In considering whether the greater attack effort is justified, it is worth remembering that the object of the attack is purely to remove two or three squadrons of Allied tactical aircraft from the battle for a short period of time. It is possible that some of the aircraft on the ground will be outside their shelters when the attack takes place, and that they will be destroyed, but this is largely incidental to the main objective of runway bombing.

In a quasi-static war situation, enemy aircraft may be held on the ground by runway bombing, but they will mostly survive to be encountered later in the conflict. Viewed in this context, it may be argued that it is not worth taking heavy losses simply to put aircraft 'on ice', hence the smaller-scale effort would be preferred. Conversely, if the enemy feels that he can pin down a wing of F-15s until the base is overrun by ground units, then it is worth paying a very high price. Even if his attrition rate is as high as 10 per cent (a figure rarely encountered historically), he can still fly six daily missions with 60 aircraft and end with a kill ratio of 2:1 in his favour, a ratio he is unlikely to achieve in air combat.

To summarize this part of the discussion, there appear to be two logical criteria in making runway cuts in a typical NATO airbase. A mission involving (say) 12–15 aircraft could be expected to make a total of four cuts, giving a residual run of approximately 2,650 ft (800 m), which would probably prevent aircraft landing, or flying ground attack missions with worthwhile loads. A mission involving 50–60 aircraft (and a small-scale re-attack) should make around 25 cuts, giving a residual run of less than 1,000 ft (300 m), and preventing most aircraft from escaping. Which type of attack the enemy would choose to conduct would depend on several considerations, including the number and type of aircraft on the base (a wing of Tornadoes being a particularly significant prize), and the possibility of overrunning the base with the aircraft still pinned on the ground.

Central European Scenario

To obtain some better appreciation of the scale of the threat to NATO airfields, it is necessary to consider how many airfields the Warsaw Pact might find it essential to attack, and how many sorties might be generated for this purpose.

In West Germany there are approximately 27 main operating bases equipped with combat and reconnaissance aircraft. The German *Luftwaffe* would represent around 15 essential targets: Bremgarten, Büchel, Fürstenfeldbruck, Husum, Jever, Lechfeld, Leck, Memmingen, Neuburg, Nörvenich, Oldenburg, Pferdsfeld, Rheine-Hopsten, and Wittmund. To this total the German *Marineflieger* might add Eggebeck, Schleswig and Jagel. The USAF operates combat aircraft from five bases in Germany: Bitburg, Hahn, Ramstein, Spangdahlen, and Zweibrücken. The RAF operates from Brüggen, Gütersloh, Laarbruch and Wildenrath, although Gütersloh is the Harrier base and thus represents a hopeless target for runway bombing in the context of precluding combat aircraft operations. The Canadian Armed Forces use Baden-Söllingen. There would thus be something approaching 30 important airbase targets in West Germany alone, when allowance is made for combat aircraft diverting to other large airfields.

If the Warsaw Pact was intent on crushing tactical air opposition for a thrust across the North German plain toward the Channel ports, then combat aircraft bases in the Low Countries would probably also be attacked in the first day or two. Belgium has four principal bases: Beauvechain, Bierset, Florennes, and

The Panavia Tornado is one of NATO's most important air assets, the 'clean' example seen here being an F.3 air defence variant. In common with the interdictor strike (IDS) version, the Tornado interceptor is equipped with thrust-reversers. (*BAe*)

Kleine Brogel. The Netherlands has five: Eindhoven, Gilze-Rijen, Leeuwarden, Twenthe and Volkel, in addition to which the USAF has a fighter squadron at Soesterberg. The three 'front-line countries' on the Central Front thus have a combined total of approaching 40 airfields that the Warsaw Pact might well decide to attack in the initial phase of a war.

According to the Pentagon booklet '*Soviet Military Power, 1987*', the Warsaw Pact nations have approximately 2,550 fighter-bombers in place, a figure that with reserves is raised to 2,600 aircraft. These nations also have 3,850 tactical interceptors, 690 reconnaissance aircraft and 460 bombers. The British '*Statement on the Defence Estimates, 1986*' uses a figure of 2,650 fixed-wing tactical aircraft of the Warsaw Pact on the Central Front. For the

Currently one of the most important Soviet fighter-bombers, the Sukhoi Su-17 *Fitter* has variable-sweep wings to reduce its airfield demands. (*USN*)

The MiG-27 *Flogger* is probably the Russians' closest equivalent to the F-4 Phantom in the supersonic fighter-bomber category. Derived from the MiG-23 air defence fighter, the MiG-27 has a pointed nose housing a laser ranger in place of the earlier radar.

The Su-24 *Fencer* is the best deep interdiction aircraft in the Soviet inventory.

outbreak of war, aircraft availability could probably be raised to almost 90 per cent, giving over 2,000 fighter-bombers.

According to the *SMP* booklet, the most common Russian ground attack aircraft is the variable-sweep Su-17 *Fitter*, of which the Soviet Air Forces have almost 900 examples. The Su-17 is reported to have a 300 nm (550 km) HI-LO-LO-HI radius with a 6,600 lb (3,000 kg) bombload and two 30 mm cannon. The next in line is the slightly heavier MiG-27 version of *Flogger*, with over 800 in Soviet service. In the same sort of mission the MiG-27 has a 325 nm (600 km) radius with the same bombload and a 23 mm Gatling-type cannon. The much larger Su-24 *Fencer* is described as 'the best deep interdiction aircraft in the Soviet inventory, with almost 800 available'. The Su-24 is believed to have a radius of 700 nm (1,300 km) in this type of sortie, with the same warload and the 23 mm Gatling gun.

It seems likely that the Su-24 (which is roughly equivalent to the F-111) would not be used in a major war for making runway cuts, since this task can be performed by far less expensive aircraft, but it might be employed to scatter hundreds of minelets over an airfield to slow runway repairs. In this context it may be recalled that at one stage (1977–1980) it was planned that the F-111 was to use the British JP233 airfield attack system. Under the designation LAAAS (Low Altitude Airfield Attack System) four JP233s would have been carried under the wings of the F-111E, giving twice the payload of the Tornado and four times that proposed for the F-16.

However, it is perhaps more likely that high-value assets such as the Su-24 would be reserved for targets other than air-fields, as would medium bombers such as the Tu-22 *Blinder* and *Backfire*, of which the Soviet Air Forces were believed in 1986 to have had 135 and 150 respectively, in addition to 200 old Tu-16 *Badgers*.

'*Soviet Military Power*' states that 'the Soviets would, under non-nuclear conditions, substitute the mass employment of aviation forces for an initial mass nuclear strike . . . in an attempt to win air superiority . . . by neutralizing the main force of enemy aviation at the onset of hostilities. The Soviet Union envisions an air operation lasting three or more days, that would involve three to seven mass strikes over the period. Two or three mass strikes would occur on the first day, with one or two additional strikes on

1960s-generation combat aircraft such as this Mirage III (exemplified by an 'R' model reconnaissance fighter) require extremely long runways, especially for landing. Until the Six-Day War of 1967, in which Israel paralysed Arab airpower on the ground in a series of pre-emptive strikes, no-one seemed to care that aircraft were parked out in the open and left totally unprotected. (*GAMD*)

subsequent days. Large strike packages, of the order of 50 to 100 aircraft, would conduct strike missions against nuclear storage depots, airfields, c^3 facilities, ports and rear area logistics and support bases.' Assaults involving up to 2,400 aircraft have already been practised in Pact exercises.

If the Warsaw Pact has 2,000 fighter-bombers available on the Central Front on the first day, these aircraft can presumably generate something approaching 6,000 sorties. To put the figure of three sorties per aircraft per day in perspective, in the 1973 Yom Kippur War Israeli aircraft flew four or five sorties per day. In strikes against North Vietnam, the USAF was generally limited to two sorties per day, but this was associated with an average mission length of around $3\frac{1}{4}$ hours, which was much longer than Communist sorties against German airfields would take. To place the suggested figure of 6,000 sorties in historical perspective, on the first day of the Normandy Invasion the Allies flew approximately 14,000 sorties in the region of the beach-head.

If the Warsaw Pact decided to restrict NATO operations at 40 key bases, then on the four-cut criterion deduced earlier this could be done with a relatively modest 600 sorties. If these attacks were

Many airfields are now equipped with hardened aircraft shelters, but these can still be destroyed by a direct hit from a conventional bomb or a variety of modern PGMs. (*BAe*)

repeated on the same day, the effort would still represent only 20 per cent of the sorties available. Only when the attacker decides to prevent aircraft escaping from a base does the effort used against airfields begin to swamp other demands. For example, if 60 sorties are flown against each of the 40 bases, with a view to 25-cut attacks, then airfield attack demands for the first day amount to 2,400 sorties, or 40 per cent of the total. When allowance is made for re-attack demands to correct missed cuts and to deal with crater repairs, then airfield attack may well become the largest single mission category, and represent half the sortie total.

The idea of very intense attacks against all the 40 main operating bases in the Central Region is somewhat difficult to accept, but it does represent an interesting extreme case. It seems more likely that the Warsaw Pact would aim to pin down the Tornadoes, Eurofighters and F-15s, and simply to disrupt operations by the less effective NATO types, an aim that might well be achieved by only 2,000 sorties on the first day. Nonetheless, it is significant that realistic Pact objectives could be achieved with the expenditure of only (say) 2,000 sorties on the first day.

However, would the Warsaw Pact really allocate one third of its fighter-bombers to airfield attacks on the first day (or two) of a conflict? As far as can be judged from published information, the keystone of NATO defensive philosophy is the use of airpower to redress the severe imbalance on the ground in terms of tanks and artillery. If the Communist hordes are to be prevented from overrunning Western Europe, then ground attack aircraft must prevent second-echelon Warsaw Pact forces from reaching the battlefront, and the forward movement of ammunition and fuel must be severely restricted. If NATO airpower can isolate the battlefront in this way, then the momentum of the Pact's armoured thrusts may be destroyed in the killing grounds that have been prepared in the decades of peace, and the Communists may be prevented from achieving significant territorial gains.

Conversely, the success of the Soviet push depends largely on the ability to paralyse Allied air efforts throughout the first few days of the conflict, and the Pact may well be prepared in consequence to devote one-third or more of the available fighter-bomber effort to airfield attacks. Although the preceding calculations are intended to produce only approximate figures, there is no doubt that the Warsaw Pact is capable of directing 2,000–3,000 sorties against NATO airfields in Central Europe on the first day of a conflict, and that (even allowing for the highest feasible attrition) such an effort would neutralize Allied ground attack missions.

It has so far been assumed for simplicity that any aircraft in the Su-17/MiG-27 category has sufficient warload-radius performance to make a single cut in a NATO runway with a high probability of success. It may be recalled that both types were credited with carrying a three-tonne load over a HI-LO-LO-HI radius of 300 nm (550 km) or more. The corresponding LO-LO radius will be approximately 175 nm (325 km) with the same load. Using modern airfield attack weapons, a cut in a runway can probably be achieved reliably with a much smaller bomb load, hence it is perhaps more realistic to consider a 215 nm (400 km) LO-LO radius with two tonnes, or 275 nm (510 km) with one tonne.

These figures are not very impressive for aircraft with maximum take-off weights in the region of 20 tonnes, but both types had their origins in air defence and are thus somewhat short of internal fuel for ground attack duties. It is also worth considering that in massed penetrations Warsaw Pact aircraft may well be able to employ HI-LO-LO-HI sorties for greater radius of action. In this case either type should be able to produce a radius of at least 300 nm (550 km) with three tonnes, 400 nm (740 km) with two tonnes, or 550 nm (1,000 km) with one tonne.

In discussing ground attack missions by around 2,000 Warsaw Pact aircraft, these would presumably involve operations from something in the region of 30 bases, while a similar number of airfields might be concerned with supporting activities. Reports indicate that there are approximately 45 Pact main operating bases within 160 nm (300 km) of the border between the two Germanies, and almost 30 more within the band 160–430 nm (300–800 km).

From the more forward bases, such as Zerbst, a 200 nm (370 km) radius covers most of Germany, and a 300 nm (555 km) radius covers half of Belgium and virtually all the Netherlands. Without considering individually all the Warsaw Pact and NATO main operating bases in the Central Region, it is impossible to say what percentage of airbases would have to be attacked in HI-LO sorties. However, assuming for the present that a one-tonne warload will suffice for a single cut, and assuming that the ground attack aircraft have the pick of forward airfields in East Germany, then most of the main operating bases in West Germany could be attacked in LO-LO sorties. Conversely, all of those in Belgium, most in the Netherlands, and some in South Germany would demand HI-LO sorties from aircraft of the Su-17/MiG-27 category.

In short, the Warsaw Pact has both the aircraft and the airfields to attack effectively all the principal NATO airbases in the Central Region, despite the fact that this would involve flying approximately 60 sorties per day against each base in order to pin aircraft on the ground. It must be emphasized that in arriving at the various bombing criteria, a late-1990s state of the art has been assumed for the airfield performance of the resident NATO aircraft, corresponding roughly to the Eurofighter, Rafale, and ATF. Most existing combat aircraft could be prevented from operating by far fewer runway cuts, requiring correspondingly less attack sorties by the Warsaw Pact.

An underside view of an
RAF Tornado, apparently
being used for tests with
the Hunting SG357
runway-piercing
submunition. (*BAe*)

4 Weapons Systems for Airfield Attack

As indicated in the second chapter, which discussed the history of airfield attacks, the growing emphasis on passive defence measures over the last 20 years has increased the relative target-value of the runways and other aircraft operating surfaces. This in turn has led to development efforts in many countries to produce special weapons that will inhibit any ground movements by aircraft, and that for survivability of the launch aircraft can be delivered in a low level high-speed pass.

The following discussion looks first at the various means to produce cuts in a paved surface, and at submunitions intended to damage taxying aircraft and other vehicles. It then considers what may be termed large-scale area weapons, which can terminate operations with a single hit.

Conventional Bombs

In WW2 runways were best attacked by heavy bombers in level flight at altitude. The height of release ensured sufficient velocity at impact to achieve a deep penetration, and a time-delay fuze gave detonation only after the bomb had passed through the paving and was deep in the soil underneath, giving upheaval over the maximum possible area. Weapon delivery accuracy was poor by modern standards, but this could be compensated by the use of a long stick of bombs, released on a heading approximately 30 degrees to the runway direction. This technique was still in use in

1982, when RAF Vulcans struck at the Port Stanley runway.

By the 1960s surface-air guided weapons (SAGW) were supposed to have ruled out straight and level bombing runs at altitude, although this did not prevent (for example) USAF B-52s from bombing Hanoi this way in the Linebacker II operation of December 1972, nor the Libyan Air Force Tu-22 making a remarkably successful medium-level attack on the runway at N'Djamena in February 1986.

The general demise of the large bomber left the task of runway attacks to smaller tactical aircraft, which compensated for their shorter sticks of bombs by making dive attacks that reduced along-track delivery errors. When dive attacks were first developed in the 1930s for the specially-built German Stukas (*Sturzkampfflugzeuge*), the intention was to achieve extreme accuracy with a single weapon against a point target. A near-vertical dive was therefore used, which simplified aiming and reduced the error in impact point to wind-drift and the ballistic dispersion of the bomb (due to manufacturing tolerances and random airflow disturbances at release).

However, the specialized Stukas were soon replaced by more conventional aircraft that employed less steep dives and compensated for along-track impact errors by using a stick of several bombs. This technique also gave effective results against linear targets such as runways. In the surprise attacks at the start of the Six-Day War of 1967, the Israelis made set-piece 40-degree dive attacks down the centrelines of the Arab runways. In the absence of surprise, such attacks simplify the task of the defences, since AAA can be sited to minimize deflection angles. A dive attack parallel to the runway centreline may also produce a line of craters that leaves a clear run on one or both sides. The modern technique is to attack at a large angle to the runway with the aim of achieving a high probability of a complete cut. Since dive bombing gives significant radar warning and long exposure to defensive fire, the ideal weapon is one that eliminates the need for a dive and somehow produces a large crater from release in a low level high speed pass.

Before discussing more advanced weapons, it may be useful as a datum to consider the effects produced by the standard HE (high explosive) bombs. Depending on the thickness of the paving and the nature of the supporting material, a 500 lb (227 kg) bomb produces upheaval over a radius of perhaps 33 ft (10 m), corresponding to an area of approximately 3,400 sq ft (315 m²). From a repair viewpoint, upheaval is the significant factor, rather than the size of the crater, since it is the concrete that is fractured by upheaval that determines the area of paving that has to be removed and repaired.

Assuming that upheaval radius is proportional to the cube-root of warhead weight, the corresponding figures for a 1,000 lb (454 kg) bomb that likewise explodes after a deep penetration are a radius of 41.5 ft (12.6 m) and an area of 5,375 sq ft (500 m²). Conversely, the Matra Durandal warhead, which weighs 220 lb (100 kg) would be expected to produce upheaval over a radius of 25 ft (7.6 m), corresponding to an area of 1,935 sq ft (180 m²). The manufacturer's brochure in fact refers to an area of destruction of 1,600–2,150 sq ft (150–200 m²).

To put these figures for upheaval radius into perspective, a NATO main runway is typically 150 ft (45 m) wide, and a conventional aircraft probably requires a width of at least 50 ft (15 m) to continue operations, although some estimates have placed this width as low as 33 ft (10 m).

It is obvious from the fact that there is only a 26 per cent increase in upheaval diameter when the warhead weight is doubled that (in achieving a runway cut) eight small bombs are better than four of twice the size, although the former case produces more drag on the aircraft. It seems logical to suppose that this argument can be extended to favour quite small warhead sizes, which presumably explains the development of the Thomson-Brandt BAP100 mentioned earlier.

'Dibber' Bombs

If, instead of piercing the runway by virtue of kinetic energy acquired in falling from altitude or in being released in a high-speed dive, a bomb is required to penetrate from a low level release, then a more complicated weapon is needed. Firstly, the bomb must not explode before the launch aircraft has achieved a safe separation distance, which means that the weapon must be retarded by a parachute or speedbrakes. Next, the bomb must strike at a reasonably steep angle, otherwise it will simply bounce off the runway. The retarding device will clearly increase the angle of descent. Thirdly, having been retarded, the bomb must penetrate, which may be done with a booster rocket.

After the 1967 Six-Day War it was reported that the Israelis had used rocket-boosted runway 'dibber' bombs, named after the garden tool for making holes in the ground. Israel Military Industries have recently stated that the bomb used was the Condib 70, now superseded by the Condib 120. Dibber-bombs were also reported to have been used in the Indo-Pakistan War of 1972, because some of the Russian bombs dropped by Indian Air Force aircraft appeared to tunnel under the ground before exploding. However, it has never been confirmed that they had rocket boost.

In the West, France appears to have taken the lead in the development of bombs that are first retarded and then accelerated to runway-piercing speeds, thus facilitating low level delivery. The *Matra Durandal* is one of the principal current runway-attack weapons, although it may also be used effectively against such targets as hardened aircraft shelters, railways, and harbour facilities. Designed in 1971 with the aim of enabling a single aircraft to disable a runway, Durandal is named after a mythological sword that could pierce stone, perhaps the French equivalent of King Arthur's Excalibur.

The Matra Durandal is 98 inches (249 cm) long, and has a body diameter of 8.8 inches (22.3 cm) and a span of 16.5 inches (42 cm) over its stabilising fins. The missile is basically cylindrical in shape, the body being made up of three functional sections in tandem. The aft section contains a two-stage parachute, the central section a rocket motor of 20,300 lb (9,200 kg) thrust and 0.45-sec burn-time, and the front section a warhead. The nose takes the form of a hemispherical aerodynamic fairing, inside which is an anti-ricochet head of wrought steel, that the brochure illustrates as a 143-degree cone.

Durandal is stressed for supersonic carriage, and for an 8.5G load factor while attached to the parent aircraft. According to the brochure, release normally takes place in a level pass at 450–600 knots (835–1,110 km/hr) at a minimum height of 250 ft (75 m). At release the weapon weighs 483 lb (219 kg). When the parachutes are jettisoned, it weighs 408 lb (185 kg). At impact the weight is down to 330 lb (150 kg). The round strikes the runway at an angle of 30–40 degrees to the horizontal, and at a speed of approximately 850 ft/sec (260 m/sec). The warhead weighs 220 lb (100 kg), and is normally set to detonate one second after impact, although a long delay can be selected to discourage runway repair efforts.

Paving as thick as 15.75 inches (40 cm) can be penetrated by Durandal. A typical crater is approximately 8.2 ft (2.5 m) in radius and 6.6 ft (2.0 m) deep, but upheaval takes place over a radius of around 24.6 ft (7.5 m). The cracking of the paving extends well beyond this, and Matra claims that a proper repair would involve replacing the paving over an area in excess of 2,700 sq ft (250 m²).

Matra sales documents refer to operational studies of runway bombing attacks against a single runway 8,000 ft (2,400 m) long and 150 ft (45 m) wide. The aim was to leave no strip of 50 ft (15 m) width that was more than 3,300 ft (1,000 m) long. The proposed tactic was to attack the runway on two oblique paths, dropping salvoes of six, eight, or ten Durandals on each track. The graphs presented appear to indicate a cut probability of approximately 65 per cent with a stick of six rounds, 75 per cent for eight, and 85 per cent for ten. The company concluded that with two successive waves (presumably meaning four sorties) 'it is almost certain that the runway will be put out of action', and that 'after such an attack, the runway would be unavailable for at least 24 hours . . . and even longer if time-delay Durandals were used.'

In considering these statements from the manufacturer in the light of the airfield attack estimates published in Chapter 3 of this book, the author would emphasize that Matra was naturally concerned with denying an airfield to today's combat aircraft, which (as noted earlier) typically require residual runway lengths of 5,000 ft (1,500 m). Since this book is concerned primarily with the case for v/STOL aircraft as the next combat aircraft generation, the runway attack criteria related to future conventional aircraft such as the Eurofighter, Rafale and ATF, that are scheduled to enter service in the mid-1990s, and in which all conceivable technological advances have been assumed in order to make these aircraft as invulnerable as possible to runway bombing. The attack effort involved is consequently of a far higher order than that necessary to deny an airfield to today's aircraft, such as the Jaguar and Phantom.

The Matra Durandal has been in series production since 1977, and is now in service with the air forces of a dozen nations. Including options, approximately 30,000 missiles have been ordered. At the end of 1985 more than 10,000 had been built, and

Matra Durandal runway-piercing weapons, mounted under a Mirage 2000. (*Matra*)

production was rising toward a planned monthly rate of 500 rounds.

In September 1983, following a three-year evaluation programme, the USAF selected the Durandal as the near-term solution to its runway-attack requirement. As purchased by the USAF under the designation BLU-107/B, Durandal reportedly has a modified braking system that will increase reliability, will be better suited to the turbulence encountered on release from the F-111, and will take the impact angle to 43 degrees to improve penetration.

Deliveries to the USAF began in late 1983, and press reports indicate that, although only 5,000 are firm at time of writing, procurement may run to 21,450 rounds over a seven-year programme. The projected cost of $681 million implies an average unit price of $31,750 in then-year dollars. It is understood that the F-4E and F-16 will each carry six Durandals, and the F-111 as many as 24.

A number of other manufacturers are developing runway-attack weapons that will function on broadly the same principles as Durandal. Spain's Expal and Brazil's Avibras are both reported to be working on accelerated bombs of the 500 lb (227 kg) class, and Egypt's Kader Factory is said to be developing a smaller weapon of around 220 lb (100 kg), which is closer to the *Thomson Brandt BAP100*.

The Matra Durandal being prepared for tests by the manufacturer. (*Matra*)

It can be argued that if the objective is simply to achieve the highest probability of a complete cut of a runway, what matters is the length of paving disrupted (i.e., the sum of the upheaval diameters) for a given weight of ordnance. Since upheaval diameter is roughly proportional to the cube root of warhead weight, small weapons are favoured. Lighter warheads presumably also reduce the separation distance required by the launch aircraft, and thus the demands on the retarding system. On the other hand, small weapons are probably less flexible in their application.

The name of Brandt is well established in the aircraft weapons field, being best known probably for the 68 mm SNEB rocket projectile, which is used by many air forces, including the RAF. In order to increase firing range and penetration capability, Brandt developed from this weapon a 100 mm rocket, which can be fired from around 20,000 ft (6,000 m) slant range, and has a destructive power comparable to that of a 155 mm artillery shell. It is available with a special demolition warhead (Type DEM) weighing 40 lb (18 kg). This DEM warhead is particularly useful against hardened aircraft shelters, being able to penetrate up to 10 ft (3.0 m) of earth and 11.8 inches (30 cm) of concrete. It was this 100 mm rocket with the DEM warhead that Thomson Brandt Armaments (to give the Company its full name) chose as the basis for its runway-attack weapon, the BAP100 (*Bombe Accélérée de Pénétration*, 100 mm).

The BAP100 functions basically in the same way as the Matra Durandal, with a braking parachute (single-stage in this case) for separation from the launch aircraft and a steep descent, followed by ignition of a rocket motor for acceleration to a suitable penetration speed. The round is 71 inches (180 cm) long, and has a diameter of 3.95 inches (100 mm). It may be carried at airspeeds up to 650 knots (1,200 km/hr) and load factors up to 7.5G, but it is normally released at 350–550 knots (650–1,020 km/hr) in straight and level flight. The original BAP100-L80 was designed for a minimum release height of 260 ft (80 m), but the recently developed BAP100-L65 reduces this limit to 215 ft (65 m). In the case of the L65, retardation has been increased through the use of a larger parachute and a reduction in round weight, and penetration has been increased by means of a modified nose ogive and a reduction in warhead diameter to 3.74 inches (95 mm).

The BAP100-L80 weighed 80 lb (36 kg), and the new -L65 approximately 72 lb (32.5 kg). At 0.5 sec after ejection, a 9.1 sq ft (0.85 m²) parachute is deployed, slowing the weapon and turning it through 50–60 degrees from the horizontal. At 2.25 sec from release the parachute is jettisoned, and at 4.25 sec the rocket motor is ignited. The motor burns for 0.3 sec, accelerating the bomb from 82 ft/sec (25 m/sec) to 755 ft/sec (230 m/sec). The warhead weighs 44 lb (20 kg) and is said to produce upheaval over an area of approximately 540 sq ft (50 m²), corresponding to a radius of 13 ft (4.0 m). Time delays up to six hours can be preset.

The BAP100 is now in service with the French Air Force and nine other services. The FAF requirement was for a 550 nm (1,020 km) Jaguar radius with 18 BAP100s on the centreline station, two drop tanks on the inboard wing pylons, and chaff/flare launchers on the outboard pylons. This is achieved with two sets of nine BAP100-L65s in tandem on the 30-6-M2 adaptor, the weight of

The standard French Air Force runway-attack load of 18 BAP100s on the centreline station of a Jaguar. (*Thomson Brandt*)

the complete armament being 1,565 lb (710 kg). This adaptor and the 18 rounds can be loaded on a Jaguar by two men within seven minutes, without any special ground support equipment. The Jaguar load can be increased to a total of 24 rounds (as was reported in the case of the Ouadi Doum attack) by placing 12 rounds on each of two adaptors of the same type, and mounting these on the inboard wing pylons, although this limits external fuel to the centreline station. With 12 L65 rounds each adaptor weighs 1,135 lb (515 kg).

An intervalometer set on the ground prior to take-off can give an impact spacing down to 20 ft (6.0 m). At a maximum release speed of 550 knots (1,020 km/hr) this corresponds to an interval of approximately 0.02 sec. It is claimed that the BAP100 system allows a single aircraft to achieve a 95 per cent probability of making a complete cut in a runway 150 ft (45 m) wide, although this estimate excludes aiming errors. It is also claimed that the 18-round load of 1,565 lb (710 kg) represents the Western world's lightest runway attack weapon system, and that four aircraft can neutralize a runway (for operations by current aircraft).

For comparison, six Durandals on two triple-ejection racks presumably weigh about 3,110 lb (1,410 kg), i.e., twice as much, occupy two pylons instead of one (the BAP100s being carried in

An RAF Tornado takes off with two Hunting Engineering JP233 runway-attack submunition dispensers under the fuselage. (*BAe*)

tandem stacks) and do not appear to give as high a probability of a single cut, judging by the manufacturers' brochures. On the other hand, the USAF reportedly felt that the Durandal could penetrate a greater depth of concrete, and could be dropped at higher airspeeds and lower heights than the BAP100-L80. The BAP100-L65 was evidently developed to answer criticism of minimum release height and penetration depth, but maximum release speed still does not meet the 600 knot (1,110 km/hr) USAF requirement.

Press reports indicate that the French Air Force would like to see further development of the BAP100 aimed at reducing minimum launch height to 165 ft (50 m). In principle the rocket motor could be ignited earlier, but this reduces the weapon's inclination to the horizontal at impact and may require a redesigned nose shape. On the other hand, if the parachute is enlarged there is a risk of aerodynamic interference with the preceding weapon, which may affect the spacing of impact points. There are thus problems in further reducing the minimum delivery height for this type of weapon, but it nonetheless seems quite possible that we may see the BAP100 cleared to 165 ft (50 m) release by the 1990s.

Submunition Dispensers

In developing an airfield attack system, Britain adopted a quite different approach from that of France. Instead of planning that a number of aircraft would each make a single cut across the paved areas, the RAF requirement evidently called for a weapon system that would allow a single aircraft to make a large number of craters, destroying the complete runway area, while minelets were dispensed to restrict repair operations.

Development of the *Hunting Engineering JP233* airfield attack system began in 1975. Flight trials of the basic submunition dispensing system (mounted on a Buccaneer) began three years later, and the first flight of JP233 on a Panavia Tornado took place in 1980. The first production order for systems for the RAF was placed in late 1982. The USAF participated in the programme from 1977 to 1980, with a view to using JP233 primarily on the F-111E and possibly the F-16. The USAF withdrew partly due to steadily rising costs in dollar terms, and partly because there was a parallel programme to develop a stand-off weapon (MRASM), although this was later cancelled.

The JP233 system was planned from the outset to give a single

The Ferranti HB876 area-denial submunition, erected and stabilized by its spring-steel legs. Its shaped charge is directed upwards to destroy any runway repair vehicle that drives over it, while its fragmenting casing disables nearby personnel. (*Ferranti*)

aircraft the greatest possible destructive power, and to suit both day and night operation, the Tornado being equipped with FLIR to AST.1010. Hunting Engineering was made prime contractor for the JP233 and the runway-cratering SG357 submunition, while Ferranti was given responsibility for the HB876 minelet.

The standard load for the RAF Tornado is two JP233s side-by-side under the centre fuselage. Each JP233 consists of two dispenser bays in tandem, the forward section containing 215 minelets and the rear section 30 runway-penetrators. The JP233 has a depth of 23.6 inches (60 cm). The front bay is 97.25 inches (247 cm) long and 33 inches (84 cm) wide, and the rear bay is 158.5 inches (402.5 cm) long and 44.9 inches (114 cm) wide. Their respective weights are 2,392 lb (1,085 kg) and 2,756 lb (1,250 kg),

A Hunting Engineering artist's impression of a JP233 attack, giving a line of craters and a scattering of area-denial weapons. (*Hunting Engineering*)

giving a combined weight of 5,150 lb (2,335 kg). Overall length is 257.9 inches (655 cm). Whereas the Tornado carries two under the fuselage, the F-111E was to have carried four JP233s under the wings, and the F-16 was to have had a single JP233 split into two modules (with revised nose and tail fairings), the SG357 unit weighing 3,021 lb (1,370 kg) and the HB876 unit 2,536 lb (1,150 kg). The two modules would have been mounted on wing pylons.

The Ferranti HB876 submunition is 5.9 inches (150 mm) long and 3.94 inches (100 mm) in diameter. It weighs approximately 5.5 lb (2.5 kg). These area-denial minelets are housed in a light alloy dispenser containing a total of 90 tubes, each tube holding one, two or three HB876s. The tubes are mounted at 90 degrees to the centreline, and canted outboard at 15 or 35 degrees to the vertical. After being ejected by cartridges, each HB876 is stabilized by a drogue, then retarded by a parachute. On landing and coming to rest, the minelet is erected by means of spring-steel legs. The upper surface forms a Misznay-Schardin plate, a concave form that produces a self-forging high velocity slug when the warhead underneath is detonated. The cylindrical casing produces fragments that are effective against both personnel and parked aircraft. The minelet has an influence fuze, and provisions for a preset delay.

The Hunting Engineering SG357 runway-cratering sub-munition might be described as bottle-shaped. It is 35 inches (89 cm) long with the impact sensor stowed, 7.1 inches (18 cm) in body diameter, and has a span of 10 inches (25.4 cm) over the fins. The SG357s are carried nose-up in a light alloy container, in tubes that are in plan-view parallel to the centreline, but canted 30 degrees below the horizontal. They are ejected downwards by cartridge-operated rams, breaking out through a frangible cover. Stabilized initially by four fins, they are retarded by parachutes, which also provide a satisfactory impact angle. On striking the ground, a crush switch on the impact sensor detonates the primary warhead, a shaped charge that blows a hole in the paving. The secondary warhead falls through this hole and detonates below the concrete.

Typical release conditions are reported to be 500 knots (925 km/hr) and a height of less than 200 ft (60 m). This height undoubtedly compares well with the figures for Durandal and the BAP100-L65, presumably because the SG357 does not require height to accelerate to penetration velocity, but the release speed quoted is lower than for the French attack systems. The length of the stick can be selected in flight from two possible values, to suit attacks along or across a runway. After firing, the JP233 is jettisoned automatically.

No data have been published on the upheaval radius produced by the SG357, though its weight of 57 lb (26 kg) suggests similar results to those of the BAP100. This being the case, its effectiveness in along-runway attacks would appear to depend on some random lateral scattering. As a means to produce a single cut across a runway, even one JP233 is a heavy weapon, but if its 30 SG357s can cut both the runway and the taxyway with a single stick, then it is a lighter system than two sticks of (say) six

Durandals each. It must also be emphasized that the weight of the JP233 includes the 215 area-denial minelets, which may well determine the period for which the runway is out of action. In this context it may be noted that the HB876 minelet is designed so that, if the enemy should attempt to clear it with a bulldozer, the minelet will topple toward the vehicle prior to detonation. The self-forging slug passes straight through the scraper blade and has sufficient residual energy to destroy the engine of the vehicle, immobilising it on the runway.

Secondary damage is provided by pre-formed dimples in the steel casing of the minelet, which on detonation form self-forging high velocity fragments that are effective against personnel, soft-skinned vehicles and aircraft over a considerable radius.

It has been reported that the production contract placed in December 1982 for JP233s was worth approximately £300 million, making this the largest order for a conventional munition to be placed by the RAF since the end of WW2.

To digress, there is some uncertainty as to how quickly bomb craters can be repaired, but the Falklands experience of 1982 showed that modern mines can be very effective in denying the use of selected areas to both personnel and vehicles. It follows that there is a case for considering a very simple dispenser-pod, which can distribute minelets over an airfield. One such weapon (based on JP233 technology) is the *Hunting Hades* area denial system, which is in effect a variant of the well-known Hunting BL755 anti-armour cluster bomb, modified to hold 49 of the HB876 submunitions used in the JP233.

Like Britain's RAF, the German Air Force funded the development of a comparatively large submunitions dispenser that would take advantage of the load-carrying capability of the Tornado and would permit attacks at extremely low level. However, in the German case the aircraft takes a single multi-purpose dispenser, the *MW-1 (Mehrzweckwaffe-Eins)*, which is manufactured by Raketen Technik GmbH (RTG), a subsidiary of MBB and Diehl. The MW-1 is now in service with the German Air Force, and is also being delivered to the Italian Air Force, likewise for use on Tornado.

The dispenser consists of a four-module container housing a total of 112 horizontal tubes. Pairs of submunitions are placed in these tubes, and ejected by cartridges at pre-selected intervals and velocities to give a uniform impact density. The empty container is then jettisoned. The MW-1 is designed to attack two types of targets: armoured mechanised formations, which are designated HZG I (*Hauptzielgruppe 1*), and airfields, known as HZG II.

The principal anti-airfield submunitions are the STABO and MUSPA. The first (*STArtbahnBOmbe*) is a cylindrical 132 mm runway-cratering weapon, with a parachute and a shaped charge for runway penetration. The second (*MUlti-Splitter Wirkkörper PAssiv*) is a sensor-activated minelet intended to destroy aircraft taxying or taking off.

Secondary submunitions are MUSA and ASW. The former (*MUlti-Splitter Wirkkörper Activ*) is a fragmentation bomblet that explodes on impact. The latter (*Anti-Shelter Wirkkörper*) is a tandem-

Underside view of a Tornado with its MW-1 dispensing a variety of submunitions. (*MBB*)

warhead submunition for use against aircraft in hardened shelters.

Deliveries of the MW-1 with the HZG-I submunitions began in November 1984, following signature of the first production contract in July that year. However, it was not until the end of 1985 that development of the HZG-II system was completed. Deliveries to the German Air Force were then scheduled to begin in 1987.

Both the JP233 and the MW-1 were designed specifically for use on the Tornado, and they are such large, heavy systems that few other aircraft could accept them without a major redesign of the dispenser modules. However, the submunitions that have appeared as a result of these developments may well find

A *Luftwaffe* Tornado in high-speed configuration, carrying the MW-1 submunition-dispenser under the fuselage. (*MBB*)

The MUSPA submunition, a passive mine with a sensor-fuzed system actuated by adjacent aircraft or ground vehicles. (*MBB*)

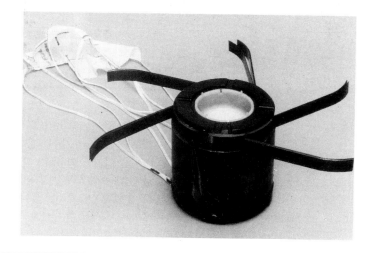

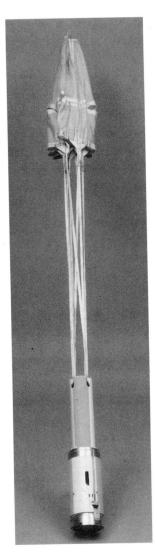

The STABO runway-attack bomblet with stabilising parachute. (*MBB*)

applications elsewhere, and this is particularly true for the Ferranti HB876 minelet and the RTG STABO runway-cratering device.

By the same token the JP233 and MW-1 may be used in conjunction with other submunitions. For example, there have been suggestions that the JP233 would be more attractive to the USAF if the Hunting SG357 were to be replaced with the Avco BLU-106/BKEP (Bomb, Kinetic Energy Penetrator). This weapon is understood to be a 100 mm projectile with a parachute that pitches it down to 65 degrees below the horizontal, and a rocket boost motor that accelerates it to runway-piercing speed, so that it can explode below the paving. The BKEP is reported to be a leading candidate to replace the Durandal in USAF service.

Stand-Off Attacks

One of the main lessons of the Falklands conflict was that traditional bombs and rockets, which require the launch aircraft to overfly its target, result in comparatively high attrition. In the postwar decades a great deal of effort has been expended in the development of surface-air missiles (SAMS) and radar-direct AAA. It may consequently be argued that it is fundamentally wrong to depend on EW and defence-suppression to allow the continued use of air-surface weapons from an earlier era, when faced with air defence systems developed specifically to decimate such attacks.

A handful of air forces have enjoyed a limited stand-off capability for some years, although the ranges involved in weapon delivery have been comparatively short, and not all these systems are suitable for airfield attack.

The *laser-guided bomb* (LGB) series developed under the *Paveway* designation by Texas Instruments had its operational debut in Vietnam in 1968, and over the next five years around 25,000 were used, destroying 18,000 targets. The Paveway I achieved a CEP of less than 20 ft (6 m), and it used to be claimed that 100 hard targets could be knocked out with 100 LGB Mk 82s, compared to 20,900 unguided Mk 82s with manual release, or 4,000 with computer-release. The contrast was less dramatic for soft targets.

However, the original emphasis was on achieving precise weapon delivery against difficult targets (such as bridges), rather than on making the attacking aircraft immune from target defences. The bomb was normally released in a 30-degree dive from a maximum distance of approximately 3.9 nm (5,500 m) at a height of 16,000 ft (5,000 m). This kept the aircraft well outside the range of 23 mm AAA and the SA-7, although it passed within reach of 57 mm AAA on the recovery. The weapon homed on to reflected laser energy from the target, which was designated (illuminated) by another aircraft using a Pave Spike pod or a Martin Marietta AVQ-9 laser in the rear cockpit.

Subsequently the *Paveway II* was developed with flip-out wings and a forward-toss delivery capability from a low approach. During the Falklands conflict there was a proposal to close the runway at Port Stanley by marking a central aim-point with an AVQ-9 in the rear cockpit of a Two-Seat Harrier, while a Harrier GR.3 tossed a Paveway II at it. Press reports at the time indicated that this weapon has a range of approximately 3.5 nm (6.5 km) from a 550 knot (1,020 km/hr) release from a climb angle of 30 degrees. However, the conflict ended before suitable means became available to mark the runway for bombing. It may also be noted that the RAF uses only the 1,000 lb (454 kg) Mk 13/18 version, but the USAF has Paveway versions of the Mk 82, 83 and 84, ranging from 500 lb (227 kg) to 2,000 lb (907 kg). Although the British version of Paveway II might have sufficed for the Port Stanley runway, to cut a standard NATO runway might take the equivalent of the Mk 84, which presumably gives an unpheaval radius of around 52 ft (16 m).

Further developments of the Paveway II have taken two forms. The US Navy *Skipper II* is basically a Paveway II Mk 83 bomb with the Shrike Mk 78 rocket motor, giving roughly three times the stand-off distance. The USAF *Paveway III* low level LGB (LLLGB) or GBU-24A/B has bigger wings and an autopilot for midcourse guidance, and is suitable for low level and off-axis attacks.

Achieving a worthwhile stand-off distance from low-level launch clearly requires both aerodynamic lift and propulsion. The basic *Rockwell GBU-15(V)* is based on the Mk 84 bomb and weighs around 2,500 lb (1,134 kg). It began life with TV guidance, although an IR version was introduced at a later stage. As an alternative to the standard Mk 84 warhead, it can take the SUU-54 dispenser, which with BLU-63 submunitions becomes the CBU-75. The GBU-15 glide bomb achieves a range of 5.0 nm (9.25 km) from less than 200 ft (60 m), or twice this distance from a height of 10,000 ft (3,000 m).

Laser-guided bombs with
flip-out fins now offer the
prospect of precise attacks
with worthwhile standoff
capability. In this photo a
Mirage 2000 releases a
1,000 kg Matra BGL.
(*CEV Cazaux*)

Fitted with rocket boost and radar altimeter, the GBU-15 becomes the *Rockwell AGM-130A*, which can achieve a range of 15 nm (28 km) from a low level launch. Modified for airfield attack, it becomes the AGM-130B with 15 BKEPs and 75 HB876s.

It may be that fly-over weapon systems such as the JP233 and MW-1 will be superseded with stand-off attack systems such as the AGM-130, but the submunitions developed for the former generation will remain applicable to the latter. All the principal submunitions are basically cylindrical, ranging in size from the 100 mm HB876 minelet to the 132 mm STABO and 180 mm SG357 runway-piercing rounds. They all lend themselves to high-density stowage in a honeycomb of launch tubes that is conveniently housed in a rectangular-section container. The indications are that we shall see firstly a short-range unpowered dispenser with stabilising fins and possibly flip-out wings, with a simple guidance system. Such weapons will provide a useful forward toss capability, perhaps without a pull-up by the launch aircraft. As a second phase, a dispenser with flip-out wings will be given some form of sustainer motor (either a rocket or a small turbine engine) and a more sophisticated guidance system to suit longer ranges.

Postscript: Both the USN Skipper and the USAF AGM-130 programmes have been deleted from the FY89 budget requests, but these projects remain useful indicators of the lines that Soviet weaponry may be taking.

Several companies are already working on unpowered free-flight dispensers. For example, *Brandt* is developing as a private venture the *BM.1200* stand-off cluster bomb, which is expected to eventuate as a family of modular weapons in the 2,200–2,650 lb (1,000–1,200 kg) class. This system derives from the 840 lb (380 kg) BM.400 modular bomb, in which three retarded 320 mm modules are expelled from the bomb casing at preset intervals from release, giving a line of high-fragmentation explosions on the ground. The BM.400 can be released in a level pass at 165 ft (50 m) and 560 knots (1,040 km/hr), or in a climbing toss attack to eliminate the need to overfly the target. The aim of the BM.1200 series is to develop this concept to allow a wide range of payloads. One proposal would provide for two modules with a total of 14 BAP100 runway-cratering bombs, while another would have 204 area-denial minelets of unspecified type.

Illustrating other possible developments in this field, Britain could have had a limited stand-off capability some years ago with the *Hunting Engineering VJ291*, although this guided cluster weapon was intended primarily for anti-armour attacks. Designed to meet AST.1227, this advanced anti-armour weapon (AAAW) was derived from BL755 cluster bomb experience, but had large folding wings at the rear. The nose fairing housed four canard surfaces that prior to launch were retracted forwards into slots. The VJ291 received target coordinates from the aircraft navigation system, making possibile the engagement of targets well removed from the aircraft track and at ranges beyond the capability of current unpowered weapons. The dual-purpose submunitions were to be dispensed centrifugally, a sensor on each allowing detonation on impact if it struck the target. Alternatively, if it landed on the ground, the device would function as a minelet. The project was cancelled in 1981.

In 1979 the USAF Armament Laboratory at Eglin AFB awarded the *Brunswick* Corp's Defense Division a contract to develop a *Low Altitude Dispenser* (LAD), and to produce nine prototypes for flight trials in 1981. These technology demonstration flights were to establish the feasibility of developing a stand-off, off-axis submunition dispenser system, to be launched from an aircraft flying below the air defence systems. The LAD was to be compatible with anti-armour, defence suppression and airfield attack missions, and with the use of the German STABO and KB44 (anti-armour) submunitions. The LAD technology demonstrator is 164 inches (417 cm) long, with a 23 inch (58.4 cm) square cross-section and a launch weight of 2,350 lb (1,065 kg) with a 1,400 lb (635 kg) payload. It has four large tailfins with trailing edge controls. The submunitions may be mounted transversely in 48 tubes of 135 mm diameter, or longitudinally in four bays on either side.

Flight tests with LAD were carried out in the speed range 325–550 knots (600–1,020 km/hr) with six types of submunition, including STABO. The system is designed for release at 100 ft (30 m), the container then falling through half that height before climbing on a preprogrammed path behind the launch aircraft to reach an altitude of 5,000 ft (1,500 m). From that height it has a maximum range of about 5.75 nm (10.7 km). It is planned that production LADS would have inertial navigation, permitting attacks on targets up to 40 degrees off boresight. A rocket motor is proposed to compensate for the low kinetic energy of the A-10 at launch, and a later, more powerful rocket would provide along-axis ranges of up to 13 nm (24.4 km), with a maximum lateral range of around 10 nm (18.5 km).

The LAD could make two runway cuts at a preselected separation. Alternatively, a strike aircraft such as the F-111 could launch up to four LADs in cross-runway attacks, each making a single cut with a very high probability of success.

Reports indicate that the USAF is funding development of a family of *Tactical Munitions Dispensers* (TMDS) for attacks against a variety of targets, with a forward toss range of around 6,500 ft (2,000 m). One form of TMD is the CBU-98/B *Direct Airfield Attack Combined Munition* (DAACM), full-scale development of which was scheduled to begin at the end of 1986. The DAACM will contain eight Avco BLU-106/B BKEPs and 24 area-denial minelets, which some reports indicate will be Ferranti HB876s. For such applications Hunting Engineering was in 1985 awarded a USAF contract to modify the HB876 to suit lateral ejection, rather than the longitudinal system used in JP233.

Various submunition dispensers are being developed on a collaborative basis. It is understood that NATO has a requirement designated LOCPOD (*LOw-Cost Powered Off-boresight Dispenser*), to deliver a cluster warhead over a range of around 10.8 nm (20 km). One LOCPUD contender is a joint effort by Brunswick in the US, Garrett Manufacturing of Canada, Agusta of Italy, and Impresa Nacional Santa Barbara and CASA of Spain, using a design based on the LAD discussed above. Another team consists of Rockwell in the US, Bristol Aerospace in Canada, Aeritalia and SNIA-BPD of Italy, and CETME of Spain. At the time of writing work on LOCFOD has been terminated in favour of the MSOW programme referred to below.

It is not clear whether the following overlaps with the LOCPOD project, but the Italian members of the second team, viz, Aeritalia and SNIA-BPD, have formed their own domestic consortium, CASMU (*Consorzio Armamenti Spendibili Multi Uso*), and displayed at Farnborough-86 a stand-off weapon-dispenser. This is projected both as a glider and as a rocket-powered vehicle, weighing 2,315 lb (1,050 kg) and 2,580 lb (1,170 kg) respectively, with a 1,640 lb (745 kg) warload. The unpowered version would have a range of up to 6.5 nm (12 km) and the rocket-powered version up to 13.5

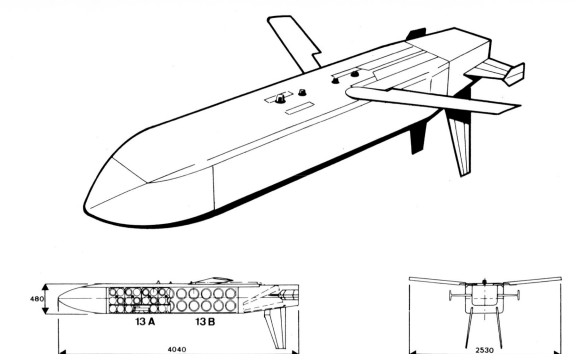

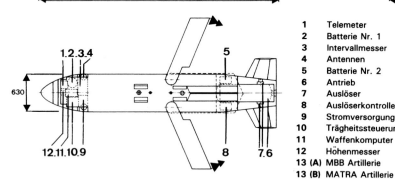

1	Telemeter	1	Telemetry (For tests)
2	Batterie Nr. 1	2	Battery 1
3	Intervallmesser	3	Intervalometer
4	Antennen	4	Antennas
5	Batterie Nr. 2	5	Battery 2
6	Antrieb	6	Propulsion
7	Auslöser	7	Actuators
8	Auslöserkontrolle	8	Actuator control
9	Stromversorgung	9	Power supply
10	Trägheitssteuerung	10	Inertial navigation
11	Waffenkomputer	11	Weapon computer
12	Höhenmesser	12	Altimeter
13 (A)	MBB Artillerie	13 (A)	MBB ordnance section
13 (B)	MATRA Artillerie	13 (B)	MATRA ordnance section

The Matra/MBB Apache/CWS stand-off attack project. (*Matra/MBB*)

A partly-sectioned view of the ASW anti-shelter submunition. (*MBB*)

The Apache/CWS weapon with wings extended. Note the use of underfins to simplify carriage on aircraft. (*Matra/MBB*)

Schematic drawing of the Franco-German MOBIDIC stand-off attack system.

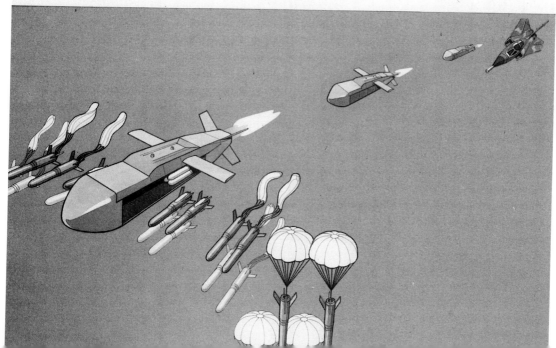

nm (25 km). Aeritalia is to develop the airframe and SNIA-BPD the rocket motor and the submunitions.

Since 1983 France and Germany have been collaborating on the development of stand-off air-ground weapons for use by both air forces. Matra and MBB are working together on the basis of earlier studies of their respective *Apache* and *CWS* (Container Weapon System). Aérospatiale and Brandt are likewise teamed with Dornier and Diehl on a weapon project designated *MoBiDic*, derived from Brandt's Pegase and the Dornier SR-SOM (short-range stand-off missile). Both these Franco-German propsals have rectangular-section dispensers with folding wings and provisions for a navigation system and sustainer motors.

Few details have been revealed of the MoBiDic project, but the Matra/MBB Apache/CWS is believed to weigh 2,200–2,550 lb (1,000–1,150 kg). The glider version is reported to have a range of up to 8.0 nm (15 km), rising to twice that distance with a solid-fuel rocket motor, and perhaps 27 nm (50 km) with a turbine engine. Development began in 1984, and the system should be available from 1989.

Cruise Missiles

Given the low fuel consumption of a gas turbine engine and fitted with appropriate navigation aids, unmanned submunition dispensers become cruise missiles. At time of writing, US, British and German companies are participating in 18-month feasibility studies of *long-range stand-off missiles* (LR-SOMS), giving ranges of up to 325 nm (600 km). In this programme British Aerospace and GEC Avionics are teamed with MBB and Boeing, while Hunting Engineering is teamed with Dornier and General Dynamics. The work is based on a Memorandum of Understanding signed on 12 July 1984, with a view to operational capability being achieved in the early 1990s.

The LR-SOM programme has been designated as one of the 'emerging technologies' under consideration by the NATO alliance to develop improved conventional weapons. The missile would be carried by British and German Tornadoes, and USAF F-15Es, B-52s, F-111s and F-16s. The feasibility study for the powerplant is being conducted by Williams International, Rolls-Royce, and KHD Luftfahrttechnik.

The Boeing-led LR-SOM would have an engine of up to 1,000 lb

(454 kg) thrust and a 1,257 lb (570 kg) payload housed in 46 tubes of 132 mm diameter. Launch weight is given as 3,500 lb (1,588 kg). The missile would have strap-down inertial navigation, with a radar altimeter for terrain-profile reference navigation and terrain-following flight control. Provisions would also be made for a Global Positioning System (GPS) receiver and for a terminal homing system.

As we go to press, it appears that the LR-SOM programme will be absorbed into the MSOW (*Modular Stand-Off Weapon*) project, which will involve seven NATO countries: the US, the UK, Canada, France, Germany, Italy and Spain.

The fact that the two LR-SOM teams are led by US companies presumably reflects the fact that these organizations already have experience of cruise missiles. The *Boeing AGM-86B* air-launched cruise missile (ALCM) entered service in December 1982 with a B-52 unit. It is powered by a Williams F107 turbofan of around 600 lb (270 kg) thrust, and has a range of over 1,350 nm (2,500 km). The ALCM weighs roughly 3,000 lb (1,360 kg), is 249 inches (632 cm) long, and has a wingspan of 144 inches (366 cm). The B-52 can carry eight ALCMs internally, and a further 12 on underwing pylons. Guidance is performed by a combination of inertial navigation and TERCOM (TERrain COntour Matching), which compares the profile of the ground with stored data. If a derivative of the ALCM were to be used for airfield attack, then terminal guidance would almost certainly be provided by DSMAC (Digital Scene-Matching Area Correlation), in which a TV image of the target as seen by the missile is compared with a digitally-stored photograph. This method makes possible an accuracy of only a few metres.

This form of guidance was also planned for the USAF *AGM-109H MRASM* (Medium-Range Air Surface Missile) version of the General Dynamics Tomahawk sea/ground-launched cruise missile, which was planned specifically for the airfield attack role. The AGM-109H was to have been an air-launched, reduced-cost derivative for use from the B-52G and F-16, with a Teledyne-CAE turbojet in place of the normal Williams turbofan, which costs three times as much. It was to have been 233 inches (592 cm) long, with a wingspan of 103 inches (262 cm) and a launch weight of 3,100 lb (1,400 kg).

The Tomahawk cruises in the region of 480 knots (890 km/hr)

and has a range of over 250 nm (450 km). Guidance for the MRASM version was to have been provided by a combination of a strapdown inertial system and TERCOM plus DSMAC. For airfield attack it was proposed to use either 28 BKEPs or 30 STABOs, with lateral ejection in either case. The BKEP was selected by the USAF in 1983, but the MRASM project was dropped in FY84.

Boeing AGM-86B air-launched cruise missile descends to low level after being released from a B-52. (*Boeing*)

Although the MRASM version of Tomahawk was abandoned, the BGM-109C Tactical Land Attack Missile, Conventional (TLAM-C) would be used against targets such as airfields. It has a launch weight of 2,800 lb (1,270 kg) and a range of 810 nm (1,500 km). Guidance uses a combination of TERCOM and DSMAC. The standard warhead is a 1,000 lb (454 kg) Bullpup unit, but a dispenser for the BLU-97/B bomblet is also planned.

The Soviet equivalent of the air-launched version of Tomahawk is the AS-15, which became operational in 1984. It has a range of the order of 1,600 nm (3,000 km) and is currently deployed with *Bear-H*, although US intelligence sources expect it to also be used on the *Blackjack*. Sea- and ground-launched versions, designated SS-NX-21 and SSC-X-4 respectively, are coming along on a slightly later timescale. A much larger cruise missile, the submarine-launched SS-NX-24 is projected for the late 1980s, and a ground-launched version of this may also appear. All these cruise missiles are expected to begin life with nuclear warheads, with conventional warheads following later in combination with improved guidance systems.

Mirage 2000N at knife-edge to display Aérospatiale ASMP nuclear missile on centreline. Matra R.550 Magic AAMs are carried on the outboard pylons for self-defence in the event of interception. (*AMD-BA*)

Ballistic Missiles

One possibility considered by the Pentagon was to attack airfields with ballistic missiles (air- or ground-launched) with conventional warheads, although there was the obvious problem that such missiles might be mistaken for nuclear weapons. The US and DOD study Counter-Air 90 envisaged the use of a ballistic missile system designated Axe, each weapon distributing runway penetration and area denial submunitions. Nor is the US alone in this approach: Soviet publications have indicated that their rocket troops would 'conduct attacks with warheads with submunitions against enemy air bases'.

America's Axe project was to have been based on the use of existing missile types, but with special warheads to suit airfield targets. One proposal envisaged the employment of obsolescent

USAF/Boeing Minuteman SSMs, modified to take conventional warheads, and based in the UK. Lockheed has studied the use of what is termed a Ballistic Offensive Suppression System (BOSS), derived from the C-4 Trident SLBM, with a warhead of 14,000 lb (6,350 kg). Another study, based on the Saturn booster, was designated TABAS (Total Air Base Attack System). A smaller weapon, named the Conventional Counter-Air Missile (CAM) was proposed by Martin Marietta, using the Pershing IA or II battlefield support missiles. In this case the payload was to have weighed 1,200 lb (545 kg) using spin-deployment of sub-munitions, but precise delivery was to be provided by radar area correlation technique. It was claimed that 100–150 CAMs would close all Pact MOBs for three days, and 500 would provide complete airfield denial.

The Russians may also have considered the use of shorter range air-launched ballistic weapons. Some years ago the US was working on JTACMS (Joint TACtical Missile System) to serve both US Army and USAF needs. In the latter case the missile, which was intended to strike at targets deep behind enemy lines, was to be launched by the B-52 and F-16. Martin Marietta's proposal was based on the T-16, a modified Patriot, while Vought proposed a T-22 Improved Lance with solid propellant motor and ring-laser gyro navigation. In the event, collaboration failed, the US Army falling back on the LTV ATACMS (Army TACtical Missile System), while the USAF went for a classified cruise missile, possibly the 200 nm (370 km) Northrop NV-150. However, as an indication of what the Soviets may be developing, it is of some interest that in the JTACMS programme Vought proposed two variants of the T-22, the one for the B-52 being 206 inches (523 cm) long and weighing 3,300 lb (1,500 kg) and that for the F-16 177 inches (450 cm) long and weighing 2,240 lb (1,015 kg). Firing ranges would have been 150 nm (280 km) and 100 nm (185 km) respectively. The improved non-nuclear warhead for Lance weighs 1,300 lb (590 kg) and distributes 825 bomblets in an area of 1,300 sq ft (400 m^2).

Nuclear and Chemical

In the event of an all-out war, NATO airfields would be targets for nuclear surface-surface missiles. There are two principal categories of SSMs that would be employed in tactical airfield attacks. Over very short ranges the Soviets might use the 65 nm

(120 km) SS-21 *Scarab*, which began replacing the 40 nm (70 km) unguided FROG (Free Rocket Over Ground) in the early 1980s. In 1985 there were estimated to be some 375 FROG and SS-21 launchers opposite NATO. Over more normal ranges airfields might be attacked by means of the 160 nm (300 km) *Scud-B* or its replacement, the 270 nm (500 km) SS-23 *Spider*, which entered service in 1985, when 500 *Scuds* launchers were opposite NATO.

Aside from their nuclear role, these ballistic missiles could also be used to carry out chemical attacks on airfields. *Soviet Military Power 1987* illustrates the ground contamination pattern that could be produced by a *Scud-B* on a military airbase. The fallout takes the form of a long elliptical footprint that typically begins some 2,800 ft (850 m) from the position of the airburst and extends downwind perhaps 13,000 ft (4,000 m) with a maximum width of almost 2,000 ft (600 m). These figures refer to a windspeed of 3 ft/sec (0.9 m/sec). The long elliptical contamination pattern of a chemical warhead airburst is well suited to the layout of a typical NATO airbase. As this document emphasizes, 'Operational flights from contaminated runways are extremely hazardous and difficult. In a Soviet chemical attack against a NATO airbase, many *Scud* missiles would be used to ensure coverage.'

The willingness of the Soviets to employ chemical weapons in Afghanistan and to supply chemical warfare equipment to favoured Arab nations and to Vietnam (whose forces have used CW in Laos and Cambodia) are evidence of the likelihood of the threat of chemical attacks against NATO airfields. Following the end of WW2, the Soviets removed from Germany stocks of the latest nerve gases and plants for their production. In subsequent years new types of chemical weapons have been developed, produced and stockpiled. Virtually all Soviet conventional weapons systems have compatible chemical warheads, and the doctrine for their use is known to include employment against airfields. Although currently less of a threat, the possibility of the Soviets using biological weapons is indicated by the anthrax accident near Sverdlovsk in 1979 and by the use of mycotoxins in Afghanistan and SE Asia.

Summary

The only sure way to make a complete cut of a wide runway with conventional weapons is to create a series of craters by detonating

A Pentagon artist's impression of a Soviet ballistic missile launch.

warheads below the paving, in order to produce the greatest possible upheaval diameter. Since this diameter is proportional to the cube root of warhead weight, it pays to use a large number of small warheads (for a given total payload on the launch aircraft).

France has taken the lead with small runway-piercing bombs that can be delivered from a low level pass, exemplified by the Matra Durandal and the even smaller Brandt BAP100. Safe low level delivery means a retarded store, which can then penetrate the concrete either by means of a rocket accelerator or a tandem warhead. The latter blows a hole in the paving with a shaped charge and then falls through to detonate underneath.

Several countries have already developed runway-piercing submunitions (e.g., SG357, STABO and BKEP), which in the first instance are mostly to be dropped from dispensers attached to the attacking aircraft. For the 1990s the emphasis is on winged and (later) powered dispensers that will provide a stand-off attack capability. Over longer ranges the same terminal effects may be achieved using turbine-engined cruise missiles with much more sophisticated guidance systems. Consideration is also being given to ground- and air-launched ballistic missiles against airfield targets.

Advanced systems for airfield attack have been under development since the early 1970s, and there appear to be no major problems to be overcome, although several of the current stand-off dispensers being developed by NATO countries may well be abandoned in favour of a multi-national collaborative programme. The Soviets may not be developing all the attack categories discussed above, but they are certainly well established with cruise missiles, and they have indicated that they would use ground-launched ballistic missiles with submunition warheads against airfield targets. There is no reason to suppose that they are not developing air-launched stand-off missiles with runway-piercing and area-denial submunitions. They obviously have ample means to deliver both nuclear and chemical warheads.

The threat to NATO airfields is thus a very serious one, and the only complete answer is to be able to disperse a sizeable proportion of our tactical air assets away from the airfields that make them vulnerable to these advanced forms of attack.

5 A Short History of V/STOL

Strictly speaking, the description 'V/STOL' can be applied to a wide range of aircraft categories, including helicopters and even airships. In practice the term is normally restricted to high performance aircraft, currently instanced only by the British Aerospace Harrier family, the McDonnell Douglas AV-8B Harrier II, and the Yakovlev Yak-38 *Forger*. However, the term is not necessarily limited to aeroplanes that can employ jet lift. It may quite legitimately include the forthcoming Bell/Boeing-Vertol V-22 Osprey and the very promising X-wing concept, which is being explored by Sikorsky.

As with so many other branches of aerospace development, the V/STOL concept has its origins in Germany during WW2, though practical progress had to wait until the 1950s, when the real demands of V/STOL were better appreciated, gas turbine engines were far more advanced, and there was even stronger operational motivation. The Germans had begun the development of the Focke-Achgelis Fa 269 air defence fighter, which was to have had a centrally-mounted BMW 801 piston engine and two tilting pusher propellers, and was intended to protect merchant ships supporting long-range submarine operations. They also developed the tail-sitting, rocket-powered Bachem Ba 349 *Natter* (Adder), which returned to earth by parachute, the pilot descending separately. Whereas the Fa 269 was abandoned in 1943 following an Allied air raid that destroyed the prototype and

The Rolls-Royce 'Flying Bedstead' of 1953 was powered by two Nene turbojets mounted back-to-back, with 90-degree bends in their jetpipes. (R-R)

most of the drawings, the Ba 349 was flown in pre-series form, although it never saw active service. Reports indicate that 200 were ordered, including 150 for the SS, although the *Luftwaffe* (at least) abandoned the project in favour of the relatively conventional Me 263.

It was later appreciated that the tail-sitter, although possibly the simplest VTO aircraft from the designer's viewpoint, involves unnecessary pilot orientation and rearming problems, and lacks the operational flexibility associated with STOL, which (by making use of wing lift) provides genuine V/STOL aircraft with the option of a far greater disposable load. The tail-sitter concept was attractive to Germany only because extremely light rocket motors were available, and because there was an urgent need for a point defence fighter, for which a few minutes of powered flight was sufficient.

In the future, gas turbine engines may attain such high thrust/weight ratios that they can provide tail-sitters with a useful performance from VTO. Around the same timescale, automatic systems to control the aircraft in the take-off and landing phases may have reached such a high reliability that pilot orientation problems can be forgotten. In these circumstances the tail-sitter or VATOL (vertical attitude take-off and landing) aircraft may find acceptance, although it is unlikely to have the flexibility of a V/STOL aircraft.

Germany's wartime thinking on jet-powered V/STOL aircraft was not limited to the tail-sitter. In a provisional patent specification filed in 1944 by an engineer named von Wolff, reference was made to achieving lift by deflecting the propulsive jets through 'one or more lattice-like, interconnected turning vanes' (i.e., a cascade) or 'swinging, overlapping ring-shaped jetpipe segments' (a bending jetpipe). It is worthy of note that von Wolff also foresaw the use of jet deflection as a means to improve in-flight manoeuvrability. However, the specification appears to have referred only to turning devices at the rear of the engine. There was nothing to tell a designer how to produce a practical V/STOL aircraft in which jet lift was directed through the CG. Such an invention was still more than 10 years away.

Try Anything Once

During the 1950s and '60s a great deal of V/STOL development work was carried out in America, though virtually all this effort served purely to demonstrate how *not* to design such an aircraft. The challenge consisted basically of applying a great deal of thrust (a value nominally equivalent to around 120 per cent of aircraft VTO weight) in such a way that the powerplant weight did not rule out a worthwhile disposable load, and so that the propulsive force and the jet lift (and any combination of these vectors) acted through the aircraft CG. Although some useful V/STOL background work was undoubtedly done in the US, the indigenous concepts explored had only a limited potential in the context of high performance combat aircraft.

One of the driving forces behind V/STOL development has been the US Navy, which service was originally motivated by fears that CTOL jet combat aircraft would not be able to operate from carriers. The Navy funded turboprop-powered tail-sitters from Lockheed and Convair (the XFV-1 and XFY-1 respectively), both of which may have made transitions between wingborne and propellor-borne flight, but were terminated in 1956. The other American tail-sitter was the Ryan X-13, which was equipped with a Rolls-Royce Avon turbojet. The X-13 was the world's first jet-powered

The Shorts SC.1 was equipped with four RB.108 lift engines in the centre fuselage and one RB.108 in the rear for propulsion. Its first transition took place on 6 April 1960. (*Shorts*)

The X-13 in horizontal flight, having successfully completed the transition from a vertical-attitude take-off. (*Ryan*)

VATOL aircraft to make both accelerating and decelerating transitions, which it first demonstrated early in 1957.

However, the tail-sitter was clearly very limited, and attention increasingly turned to the flat-riser, which required less mental gymnastics from the pilot and could hopefully take off at much higher weights, using STO to exploit wing lift. Unfortunately, the flat-riser demanded more of an invention: the tail-sitter had been simply a highly powered conventional aircraft turned on end, but the flat-riser needed thrust that could somehow be applied either along or normal to its longitudinal datum and ideally at intermediate angles.

Aside from finding a powerplant that would provide the high thrust/weight ratio necessary for a worthwhile disposable load (and hence warload-radius performance) and would place the thrust vector through the CG over an angular range of at least 90 degrees, the designer also had to produce an aircraft that would be simple in both engineering and piloting terms. The finished product had to be not too expensive, reliable enough for operations from simply-equipped front-line sites, and sufficiently straight-forward in its handling characteristics to give problem-free conversion for ordinary squadron pilots coming from CTOL fast jets.

Three decades later the feasibility of V/STOL flying is taken for granted, simply because literally millions of people have witnessed demonstrations by Harriers. However, in the 1950s and early 1960s there was no such background knowledge, and any new airframe/engine combination represented a leap in the dark. When this writer went to NASA Langley early in 1960 to liaise with the engineers carrying out the free-flight model trials to establish the basic feasibility of the P.1127 concept, HSA had just received the first results of conventional tunnel testing in the UK, results that showed the aircraft to be catastrophically unstable longitudinally in partially jetborne flight. Having no prior experience in this field, the P.1127 suddenly appeared to us at HSA to be a hopeless project. What we did not then appreciate (though the NASA team under Marion McKinney did) was that considerable degrees of static instability could be tolerated for the brief period of transition, provided the aircraft had sufficient control power in pitch.

In attempting to design a practical flat-riser, it was basically a matter of augmenting the thrust of a turbojet in some way, and arranging for that thrust to act through the aircraft CG throughout transition. An extreme example of thrust augmentation is the helicopter rotor, driven by one or more additional turbine stages, but the blades normally place restrictions on forward speed that are not acceptable in the context of combat aircraft.

In terms of a much lower bypass ratio, General Electric promoted the use of relatively small buried fans, driven in V/STOL by the diverted exhaust gases of the propulsion engine(s). However, in their simplest form these fans (typically buried in the wings, as tested in the Ryan XV-5A) gave considerable momentum drag, since the air passing through them during STO

The Lockheed XV-4B Hummingbird was equipped with two P&W JT12 turbojets, exhausting through augmentors in the centre fuselage. The augmentation achieved proved disappointing, and the aircraft was later fitted with lift engines in place of the augmentors. N705NA is preserved at the US Army Museum, Ft Rucker, Alabama. (*Mike Verier*)

and accelerating transitions had its horizontal velocity component destroyed. Some designers proposed to avoid this problem by using vectored (tilting) fans that could be retracted into the fuselage during wing-borne flight. Nonetheless, the GE fans represented significant weight and volumetric penalties, even if the restriction on take-off speed could be eliminated.

Lockheed favoured the use of jet augmentors, specially-shaped ducts in the centre fuselage in which jets supplied with high-pressure air from the engines induced much larger amounts of the surrounding air to flow through the system. This induced air flow created suction on upward-facing surfaces, augmenting the jet lift available from the primary flow. In the laboratory augmentations of more than 50 per cent were demonstrated, but full-scale results were disappointing. The concept was employed with no great success on the Lockheed XV-4B Hummingbird and the later Rockwell XFV-12A, which had augmentor ducts in the wings and canards.

Lift Engines

An alternative approach, as favoured by Rolls-Royce, was to optimize the propulsion engine(s) for forward flight, and create all the jet lift required by adding specialized lift engines. Since these were required to function only for a few minutes during take-off and landing, they could be very simple powerplants, achieving outstanding thrust/weight ratios. At a time when conventional turbojets produced T/W values of around 4:1, lift engines rapidly improved from 8:1 to 16:1, and a ratio of 24:1 was projected for the R-R/Allison XJ99. These figures are slightly misleading, since there was a considerable increase in aircraft structure weight associated with these buried engines, but lift engines do offer a feasible solution, especially in the context of V/STOL transport aircraft. In combat aircraft they tend to result in fat fuselages with unacceptable wave drag, but they do offer the prospect of surviving an engine failure during transition, given a battery of eight or more lift engines (as in the Dassault Mirage IIIV).

At the time all these various ideas represented high-risk projects, but they warranted investigation because it was feared in the mid-1970s that NATO would lose most of its tactical bases on the first day of a European conflict. Of the ideas discussed up to this point, the only one with serious development potential appeared

The Rockwell XFV-12A was a technology demonstrator for a supersonic naval VTOL fighter using jet augmentors. It was powered by a P&W F401 turbofan, and had augmentors in the wing and foreplanes. Reports indicate that it never left the ground. (*Rockwell*)

to be the Rolls-Royce concept of separate engines for lift and propulsion. It was tested in the Shorts SC.1 and Dassault Balzac and Mirage IIIV, and further developed in Germany's EWR VJ101C, which had four small engines in rotatable wingtip pods, and two lift engines in the fuselage. The subsequent VJ101D was to have had a basically conventional airframe arrangement (rather like a small TSR.2), but with jet deflection on the two propulsion engines, augmented by five lift engines further forward.

In later Franco-German studies it seems to have been agreed that the optimum approach was to size the propulsion engines for conventional flight demands, turn their jets downwards for v/STOL, and add sufficient lift engines to achieve the necessary take-off performance. In essence, Dassault apparently accepted what had been the German philosophy for several years, although this involved abandoning the low-speed safety of the Mirage IIIV arrangement.

The multi-engine v/STOL series of projects were not without their supporters in the UK. The immensely powerful Rolls-Royce naturally favoured the use of lift engines, in which the company had established a world lead. The Government-owned Shorts Bros clearly knew more about this type of powerplant installation than any other company in the UK, and in the late 1950s was undoubtedly the leading British airframe manufacturer in the v/STOL field.

In the event, lift engines have found no application in Western v/STOL aircraft to date, although two are used in the Yak-38, balancing the rotatable thrust of the propulsion engine. This Soviet Navy aircraft might thus be regarded as a practical example of the v/STOL powerplant concept that the Germans argued for in the 1960s, and tested in the VFW 1262. That aircraft had the two lift engines split between the front and rear fuselage, and the lift/thrust engine had basically the same four-nozzle arrangement as the Harrier's Pegasus (rather than two nozzles at the back end), but the VFW 1262 was conceptually almost identical to the much later Yak-38.

Lift engines have thus found a limited practical application, but they have always had the attraction that a single engine type can be applied to a wide range of v/STOL projects, whereas the Harrier's Pegasus has only one application, which severely restricts the

TOP As an alternative to variable-sweep wings for STOL, the Soviets investigated the use of lift engines. This MiG-designed *Fantail* was shown at Domodedovo in 1967, but it was the swing-wing MiG-23 *Flogger* which entered production.

This pair of Yak-38 *Forger* naval VTOL aircraft is armed with the AA-8 *Aphid* air-air missiles. In jetborne flight the thrust from the two lift engines located just behind the cockpit is balanced by the vectored thrust from the propulsion engine.

spreading of research and development costs.

Breakthrough

What made possible a comparatively simple V/STOL combat aircraft was the invention of a new type of powerplant in which the thrust could be turned through more than 90 degrees, rotating about a point very close to the engine CG. It must be appreciated that a high performance combat aircraft conventionally has its engine(s) in the rear fuselage, balancing the weight of the pilot, cockpit and operational equipment in the front. The Bell X-14, which made its first flights and hovers in early 1957 and completed transitions on 24 May 1958, vectored its thrust roughly about the CG, but it employed von Wolff-type (i.e., cascade) jet deflection at the rear of the engines. The weight of the engines was consequently well ahead of the aircraft CG, and it was thus impossible to develop the concept directly into a high performance

combat aircraft with the cockpit well forward. One such project was drawn in the Hawker project office, using an afterburning Bristol Olympus engine, but the balance calculations were imaginative, to say the least.

The invention that led to the practical vectored-thrust engine as we know it today was the Wibault *Gyroptère*, in which a gas turbine in the rear fuselage drove four centrifugal blowers in the sides of the fuselage by means of shafts and gearboxes. The output from the blowers could be vectored by turning their casings, and four were used to create a positive ground effect between them. It was basically a heavy arrangement, but the engine was in the right place balance-wise, and the aircraft was a starting point from which something might be achieved.

Since Wibault proposed to use the 8,000 shp Bristol Orion engine, the *Gyroptère* project passed to what was then Bristol Aero Engines. The company's technical director, Dr (later Sir) Stanley Hooker, passed the problem of transforming it into a practical engine to Gordon Lewis, who later became engineering director (new business) for Rolls-Royce. Lewis rejected the idea of long shaft-drives and four separate blowers, and replaced this arrangement with a single multi-stage front fan. The efflux from the fan was ducted to two rotatable nozzles in the fuselage sides, and at a later stage the exhaust gases were likewise bifurcated to two additional rotatable nozzles, giving the 'four-poster' arrangement characteristic of the BE.53 that provided the basis for the Rolls-Royce Pegasus.

The attractions of this engine concept were that it was comparatively simple, offered the promise of a reasonably high thrust/weight ratio, and allowed all the installed thrust to be directed horizontally for acceleration in STO, then deflected down at the optimum angle for unstick and acceleration to wingborne flight. The two shafts of the engine were made to contrarotate, virtually eliminating gyroscopic effects, and making it technically feasible to fly the resulting aircraft (the P.1127 and later the Harrier) with purely manual control. The engine also supplied high pressure bleed air to reaction controls in the wingtips, nose and tail, these low-speed controls being linked directly to the tailplane, ailerons and rudder, so that the control column and rudder bar continued to function in the normal sense.

The BE.53 brochure had been passed to Hawker Aircraft in mid-

The Bell X-14 was probably the world's first successful vectored-thrust V/STOL demonstrator. Vectoring was achieved by means of two sets of cascades behind either engine. The first cascade was fixed, turning the jet through 45 degrees, and the second could be rotated to turn the jet either back to the horizontal or down to the vertical. (*NASA*)

1957. The company's chief designer was the late Sir Sydney Camm, who handed the project to Ralph Hooper, later chief engineer at British Aerospace's Kingston plant. Hooper made various contributions to the conceptual development of the BE.53, and was the project engineer in charge of P.1127 development from 1957 to 1965, when the P.1127(RAF) version was ordered into production as the Harrier.

The fundamental advantages of the single vectored-thrust engine have been discussed already. The fundamental disadvantage in performance terms, relative to the multi-engined aircraft the Germans were advocating, was that cruise fuel consumption was very high. The Germans chose their lift/thrust engines to suit cruise demands precisely, hence SFC (specific fuel consumption, i.e., the fuel flow rate per unit thrust) was as low as it could possibly be. In contrast, the single vectored-thrust engine was optimized for a high static thrust/weight ratio. Pressure ratio was consequently low, and when this massive engine was throttled back for cruise, the SFC curve went straight through the top of the brochure.

A secondary disadvantage of this approach was the spillage drag associated with the oversize intake, which had to be large enough to ensure a high pressure recovery at full throttle at low speeds, but was consequently far larger than was required by the cruise mass flow.

In fairness it must be added that Rolls-Royce later improved the cruise SFC of the Pegasus, though it remained far higher than that for a cruise-optimised engine such as the Turbo-Union RB.199. The single Pegasus-type engine nonetheless had the advantage that in combat a great deal of thrust was available, especially at low speeds. This was later to prove useful when thrust-vectoring in forward flight (VIFF) was employed by AV-8As and Sea Harriers in mock combat with conventional aircraft. The VIFF technique is basically a last-ditch manoeuvre to force an attacker to overshoot, but it involves considerable loss of speed, and thus depends on the aircraft having a large thrust available to regain manoeuvring speed. The Harrier's reaction control system, which comes into operation whenever the four nozzles are lowered beyond 20 degrees, is also useful in maintaining attitude control in conventional dogfights that lead to very low airspeeds.

It must also be emphasized that the Harrier/Pegasus

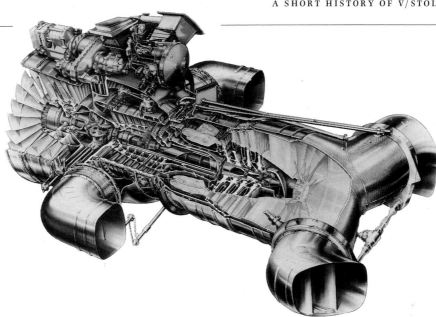

Cutaway drawing of the Rolls-Royce Pegasus (F402) as developed for the AV-8B Harrier II. It is distinguished from earlier models by the zero-scarf front nozzles, which reduce lateral splay of the jets. (R-R)

arrangement is one of the few V/STOL concepts that can make use of jet lift in high-speed combat. To the best of this writer's knowledge, there was never any suggestion that (for example) the Mirage IIIV or the VJ101D could improve their manoeuvrability or deceleration in this way, and it appears extremely unlikely that the Yak-38 has such a facility.

In the context of the fundamental advantages and disadvantages of the single-engine approach to V/STOL, it is clear that safety (especially in the hover or in partially jetborne flight) had to be an important consideration. The view at Hawker was that there were two possible ways to achieve a reasonable safety level: the single-engined aircraft and the original Rolls-Royce concept, in which the aircraft weight was supported by a large number of lift engines grouped together around the CG. What was not acceptable was the German concept, in which lift engines and lift/thrust engines were distributed around the aircraft, so that a failure at one extremity had to be counterbalanced by cutting back an engine at the other.

Since in the Hawker view a multiplicity of lift engines was incompatible with front-line operations, the single engined concept was essential. It is not always appreciated by aviation historians that Sir Sydney Camm turned down all kinds of multi-engined V/STOL projects, before the Bristol engine and Hooper's P.1127 came along. Once that concept was accepted, there was no doubt in anyone's mind at Kingston that its success depended critically on the dependability of the BE.53 (Pegasus). Although two Pegasus engines were flown in the Dornier Do 31, the world's first V/STOL transport aircraft, the production version was to have had the far more economical Spey. It followed that engine hours would build up only slowly, and if a Pegasus failed it would do so in a P.1127 or Harrier.

In the circumstances, and bearing in mind that the Pegasus was given a remarkably high short-term thrust rating for V/STOL, the engine performed far more dependably than some of us feared. It is true that the Harrier accident rate for the first few years was extremely high, but the main engine-related accident category was compressor surge due to birdstrikes, which were common as a result of the RAF's low level operations and the size of the intakes. The effective capture area was increased by the tendency of birds to strike the sides of the front fuselage and ricochet into the intakes. However, the ability to achieve a relight was significantly enhanced by the addition of a manual fuel control system. On the whole the Pegasus has performed extremely well, justifying Hawker's gamble on a single engined V/STOL project.

There were some early one-off accidents due to powerplant problems, but these were solved long before the first production aircraft appeared. Soon after the first transitions (on 28 October 1961), the second prototype P.1127 was lost when the front left-hand nozzle (then made of fibreglass) detached, producing an uncontrollable rolling moment when the flaps were lowered. Almost a year later the first development batch aircraft was written off, following a titanium fire in the HP compressor due to inadequate blade clearances under 'G'. In the following year the first prototype made an extremely heavy landing during its demonstration at the Paris Air Show, apparently due to a piece of grit jamming a valve in the pneumatic system that controlled the angular position of the four nozzles. Such faults were quickly corrected: the front nozzles became stainless steel, blade clearances were increased, and a filter was added to the nozzle rotation system.

In terms of handling characteristics in partially jetborne flight the P.1127 was relatively straightforward, although some pundits outside the company felt that the swept wing, which had to be mounted very high to clear the bulk of the engine, would give an unacceptable dihedral effect (i.e., rolling moment due to sideslip) in transition. It is true that the deflected jets increase dihedral effect, but this was not in itself a major problem. The real difficulty was that at low speeds the momentum drag of the intakes decreased weathercock stability. This effect tended to increase sideslip angle, which could (if unchecked) generate a rolling moment greater than the power of the lateral controls.

Recognising this danger, the company installed a yaw vane ahead of the windscreen, and instructed pilots to minimize sideslip in transition. Unfortunately, in 1969 there was a fatal accident when the pilot of a Harrier, taking off into the sun, apparently allowed sideslip to build up, and the aircraft rolled out of control. As a result, the Harrier was given a yaw autostabilizer, a head-up display of lateral acceleration, and a rudder pedal shaker that in effect required the pilot to 'stamp out the vibration'.

In other respects the Harrier proved vice-free, although the two-seat derivative was problematical in directional stability in conventional flight. For reasons that were never fully understood, the trainer runs out of stability (i.e., yawing moment due to sideslip) above 15 degrees of AOA. When this was corrected by means of an oversize fin, the aircraft proved to be too stiff directionally at low AOA, making weapon-aiming difficult, particularly in gusts. The aircraft thus reverted to the fin of the single-seater, relying on an AOA limit and on partial airbrake extension at low speeds.

The fundamental pros and cons of the single vectored-thrust engine and the few technical problems of the P.1127/Harrier series have been discussed in some detail to prove the point that the P.1127 was a good choice for a V/STOL technology demonstrator for the 1957 timeframe. Many experts feel that the single vectored-thrust engine is still the right way to go, although others would argue that the major advance in powerplant reliability over the last 30 years considerably strengthens the case for multi-engined V/STOL projects, especially in the context of strike fighters, which benefit more from a cruise-matched powerplant.

The Big Twin

The point is also worth making, that a single-engined aircraft is limited in size. Few designers would suggest such an aircraft as a V/STOL replacement for the F-15 or F-111. In the early 1960s, when

Hawker (on orders from MOD) was trying to design a P.1154 that would be acceptable to both the RAF and RN (the latter being intent on acquiring the F-4), the project office considered a twin-Spey version as an alternative to the single BS.100 engine. In this writer's view there was no significant difference between the two options, but the weight estimates were revised to show the twin-Spey version to be considerably heavier, arguably because the company had no wish to develop such an aircraft.

Although the twin-Spey P.1154 would presumably have saved on engine R&D costs, it would not have given the RN the overwater safety it desired. In the event of one Spey failing, the aircraft could have returned to the carrier on the thrust of the other, but there was no way for it to land. Each engine had two nozzles, with cross-over ducts at the rear to minimize rolling moments if one failed at the hover. However, one engine simply could not provide sufficient jet lift, even for a conventional naval landing. The pilot would have had to return to the battle group and eject where he could be rescued.

The lesson to be learned from the experience of the twin-Spey P.1154 is that a pair of vectored thrust engines is conceptually little different from the single-engined arrangement so far developed. If suitable engines already exist, the twin approach may save money. However, it *may* produce an aircraft with more frequent engine failures, and in the event of one failing it *may* not provide the ability to save the aircraft.

Cost-Cutting

Those who were subsequently concerned with Harrier marketing suspected that, if the vectored-thrust front-fan engine had been invented in the US, it would have found large-scale application in the combat aircraft of the 1970s. Instead, the idea (having originated in somewhat impractical form in France) was developed in the UK. In consequence, the first two decades of V/STOL progress were characterized by half-hearted support by Government and MOD, and tight financial restrictions on any attempt to

Model portraying the Hawker Siddeley Aviation P.1154 supersonic V/STOL project in its element. (*HSA*)

improve the hardware. The quantum leap in performance provided by the McDonnell Douglas AV-8B Harrier II was due only in part to the superior technology of the American manufacturer (MDC undoubtedly being far ahead of BAe in the use of advanced composites); a great deal of the improvement was due to the fact that there had been no funding for V/STOL performance enhancement since 1971.

The P.1127 began as a Hawker-funded project study in 1957, and in the following year the first details were drawn. Also in 1958 the BE.53 engine went ahead, with 75 per cent of the funds provided by America's MWDP (Mutual Weapons Development Program) and the remainder by Bristol. Air Ministry declared that, since the project was subsonic, it had no interest, and no intention of funding it. In the following March Hawker committed itself to the production of two prototypes. Finally, on 22 June 1960, four months before the first P.1127 carried out its initial hover, the two prototypes were officially funded.

The basis for this long-delayed support was a draft operational requirement (GOR.345) for a Hunter replacement, which was first circulated in April 1959, but was withdrawn in late 1961. Eventually Britain funded the two P.1127 prototypes and four development batch aircraft, and a share of the nine Kestrels (slightly improved P.1127s) that carried out the first V/STOL operational trials in 1965 under joint US/UK/German auspices.

However, the P.1127 and Kestrel were purely V/STOL technology demonstrators, intended to show that the single vectored-thrust

The Dassault Balzac was a technology demonstrator for a supersonic strike fighter equipped with a composite powerplant of lift and propulsion engines. (*GAMD*)

engine was the right way to go. Although company spokesmen were fond of saying that the P.1127 was 'designed from the outset for the combat role', all this meant was that it had a 7.5G structure. Even the Kestrel, with two pylons and a reflector sight, had no real operational capability.

Indeed, there was no reason for the P.1127 to be anything more than a technology demonstrator, since in late 1961 NATO had issued a draft OR for a supersonic V/STOL strike fighter, the NBMR-3. The performance essentials were a 250 nm (465 km) LO-LO radius with a 2,000 lb (907 kg) nuclear store, taking off in a distance of 500 ft to 50 ft (150 m to 15 m). This warload-radius performance and supersonic dash capability at altitude were far beyond anything that could be achieved by straightforward P.1127 derivatives. What was needed was a much larger aircraft, with more static thrust and engine characteristics that gave proportionally far more thrust at high speeds. In the context of a single vectored-thrust engine, this implied combustion in the fan efflux, or what was termed plenum chamber burning (PCB).

The first such project, the P.1150, powered by a BE.53/6 with PCB, had been drawn by Hooper in early 1961. In due course this developed into the P.1154 with the BS.100 engine, which was submitted in early 1962. The P.1154 and the Mirage IIIV were declared joint technical winners of the NATO contest, but it was left to Britain and France to develop these projects at their own expense. France quickly became disenchanted with the Mirage IIIV. It is believed to have had some technical problems and a limited supersonic performance, but the main drawback is thought to have been the proposed operational concept, which involved frequent changes of operating sites, despite the fact that these had full support facilities.

As recorded earlier, John W Fozard (who was subsequently chief designer, Harrier, from 1965 to 1978) was appointed chief designer, P.1154, in 1963.

The HS.1170, the British contender for the VAK191 contest. Preliminary design by Roy Braybrook. (*BAe*)

The RAF was quite enthusiastic about the P.1154, which would have made it the first air force in the world to operate a supersonic V/STOL aircraft. However, the politicians of the day wanted inter-service commonality, and insisted that the P.1154 should be modified to suit RN requirements for a Sea Vixen replacement. This fatuous demand wasted two years, and in February 1965 the P.1154 was terminated on grounds of timescale and cost.

Balzac V 001

H.S.1170
LIGHTWEIGHT V/STOL
STRIKE RECONNAISSANCE

The VJ101C had two lift engines in the fuselage and four engines in rotatable pods. The 'translating' intakes made possible jet lift at quite high forward speeds. X-2 (the second aircraft) had afterburning propulsion engines and marginally exceeded Mach 1. (*EWR*)

The Dassault Mirage IIIV was the first V/STOL aircraft capable of Mach 2 in level flight. It had eight RB.162 lift engines and one SNECMA/P&W TF306 for propulsion. The Mirage IIIV first prototype is seen here at the hover. (*GAMD*)

As a consolation prize, HSA was awarded a contract to develop and produce an operational derivative of the subsonic P.1127, an aircraft with far less performance than the RAF had expected to receive. The idea of being stuck with an aircraft purely to safeguard employment at Kingston and Bristol was viewed by the RAF with something short of enthusiasm, and the service made no secret of its opposition. Every air force in the world soon knew that the RAF was being given an aircraft it did not want, and the story persisted, long after the service had grown to appreciate the operational flexibility that this form of V/STOL provided.

In essence, the rapid development of the vectored-thrust V/STOL concept to give the RAF an aircraft comparable in conventional flight to the F-4 had been abandoned, and a simple low-cost substitute had been ordered to maintain Britain's toe-hold in V/STOL for a generation, at the end of which money *might* be found to develop something more advanced.

There are various points that can be made about the 1965 decision. Firstly, this minimum-outlay policy actually did (to the surprise of many at Kingston) enable the UK to maintain a V/STOL lead for a significant period. Secondly, in terms of size and ground erosion characteristics the Harrier was far more compatible with dispersal than the much larger P.1154 with its high energy jets would have been. Thirdly, having deferred the opportunity to make a major advance with V/STOL from the 1960s to the '80s, when it came to replacing the Harrier MOD abandoned Britain's only aerospace lead and bought an American aircraft. From a short-term commercial viewpoint this was undoubtedly a good decision, since McDonnell Douglas offered extremely attractive terms. From a long-term viewpoint, the real test will be whether BAe's part in the AV-8B programme leads to a significant role in the development and production of the next generation, which will hopefully be supersonic.

The Anglo-German Programme

The key to high performance in the case of a vectored-thrust front-fan engine is PCB, and this is just as true in the context of a subsonic ground attack aircraft as for a supersonic fighter such as the P.1154

It was clear from the late 1950s that the German Air Force was a potential V/STOL operator, due to the very serious threat to its

This head-on view of the VFW1262 emphasizes the minute wing of the aircraft, which was designed only for VTO (not STO), and had no in-flight manoeuvre requirement. (*VFW Fokker*)

The Dornier Do 31, combining two Pegasus and eight lift engines (all by Rolls-Royce) was probably Germany's most successful V/STOL project, though no production order materialized. (*Dornier*)

airfields from Warsaw Pact aircraft, and since Germany was engaged in various V/STOL investigations. In 1960 the *Luftwaffe* generated a requirement for a seven-ton VTOL nuclear strike fighter, designated VAK 191, based on the predicted performance of the Focke-Wulf FW 1262. In the eyes of Hawker management and MOD (neither of which had taken on board the fact that the OR called for ten times the VTO radius that could be achieved in the early 1960s by the P.1127) this was a golden opportunity to sell the British aircraft. The fact that Germany wanted experience of developing a high performance V/STOL aircraft was ignored: they were going to be stuck with the P.1127. Without consulting the Hawker project office, MOD rubber-stamped the VAK 191 requirement as the basis for an Anglo-German development programme.

The only real hope was to demonstrate to the Germans that a high-performance single-engined design could produce a similar warload-radius performance to the three-engined, cruise-optimized FW 1262, and would be vastly superior in every other respect. On this basis they might have agreed to abandon the FW 1262 in favour of the Hawker proposal (the P.1163, redesignated HS.1170), conceivably accepting a small number of P.1127s as an interim type.

Achieving a ten-fold increase in radius of action demanded a completely new engine, with a high thrust/weight ratio and a low cruise SFC. The inevitable conclusion was that PCB had to be used, since this would give a proportionally smaller, lighter engine that was far better matched (PCB off) to cruise thrust demands. Whereas the Pegasus and the BS.100 had been engines that were convenient for Bristol to develop (on the basis of existing engine components), what was required in this case was a highly optimized powerplant, giving a larger PCB boost and lower cruise SFC than any V/STOL engine so far proposed.

Rolls-Royce (Derby) and Bristol were therefore approached with detailed proposals on how they should develop the RB.153 and the BS.94 respectively, to achieve the performance needed to meet the VAK 191 requirement. The RB.153 proved to have a development limit of 17,000 lb (7,710 kg) thrust, without a reduction gearbox, but the BS.94/5 offered the 18,500 lb (8,390 kg) that was required, and this formed the basis for the HS.1170. Relative to a developed Pegasus, it promised an increase in thrust/weight ratio from 7.0 to 8.6, and a 15 per cent improvement in cruise SFC, while allowing a 27 per cent reduction in wetted area, due partly to its much smaller diameter. The HS.1170 also had a much higher wing loading than the P.1127, since it was to operate purely in a VTOL mode, and had no manoeuvre requirement.

The BS.94/5 gave an unprecedented PCB thrust boost of 60 per cent, with a thrust-split of 4:1 between the front and rear nozzles. This moved the engine aft relative to the aircraft CG, giving longer intakes and smoothing the flow to the engine.

The HS.1170 was to have flown in 1966 and entered service in 1969, but the Anglo-German programme was thrown away by the arrogance of those responsible for the British side of the commercial negotiations. Obsessed with Hawker's success in getting the P.1127 through transitions, they insisted that (in recognition of British know-how) design royalties should be paid to Hawker, *whichever aircraft won the contest*. Germany quite naturally refused to accept this ridiculous condition, and the HS.1170 programme terminated. The FW 1262 (redesignated VFW 1262) was flown in the form of three prototypes, then abandoned. Britain ordered the P.1127 (RAF) into production as the Harrier, although this offered far less performance than the HS.1170.

Harrier and Sea Harrier

The decision to go ahead with a relatively modest development of the P.1127 was a good one in the sense that the end-product was a small aircraft with limited logistic demands and the minimum of ground erosion problems, although it is doubtful whether its grass field operational capability would ever be exploited in war.

The main faults with this minimum-cost decision were that it was associated with procurement of a relatively sophisticated nav-attack system, and that some of the basic shortcomings of the P.1127 were simply glossed over. Although the wing of the P.1127(RAF) was far better than that of the first prototype P.1127 (reflecting the half-dozen modifications tested), the cockpit was still cramped and lacked rear view, V/STOL handling still left considerable scope for improvement, and outrigger track was still embarrassingly large. There was no doubt that the Harrier required a very high standard of navigation accuracy in order to carry out low level first-pass attacks, and the Ferranti FE541 inertial system was generally accepted to perform better than the specification 2 nm (3.7 km) error per hour of flight, after a normal (12 minute) alignment. However, whether it made sense to equip this weight-critical aircraft with a head-down moving map display that had been developed for the TSR.2 is open to question.

The Harriers purchased by the RAF initially formed the OCU and four operational squadrons, one in the UK and three in Germany. However, the RAF Germany Harrier wing was in 1977 reformed as two squadrons due to a shortage of administrative accommodation, on moving forward from Wildenrath to Gütersloh, located close to the border of the two Germanies.

The Harrier was purchased by the US Marine Corps as the AV-8A (later modified to AV-8C standard), attaining operational capability in 1971, two years after the first RAF Harrier unit. Due purely to the fact that the USMC purchase was approved on a year-by-year basis, all 110 aircraft (including eight TAV-8As) were built and flown in the UK, and then broken down for delivery in USAF transport aircraft. The AV-8As had American radios and Sidewinder provisions, Stencel ejection seats in place of Martin-Bakers, and a simplified nav-attack system, but in other respects

The Marine Corps AV-8A
differed from the RAF
GR1 in having a less
sophisticated nav-attack
system and a Stencel
ejection seat. The US
version also had fixed
outboard pylons for AIM-9
missiles, and a large
tactical VHF antenna over
the centre fuselage.

RIGHT Harrier GR.1
cockpit: the cluttered
arrangement of the
instruments and controls,
and lack of visibility
(especially to the rear) is
a world away from the
Sea Harrier and AV-8B.

A line-up at Patuxent River NAS in 1979, with two AV-8As, two YAV-8B conversions, a TAV-8A two-seater, and a Learjet. (*MDC*)

BOTTOM The pointed nose of the Harrier GR.1 (shown here) soon gave way to the GR.3's 'thimble' with Ferranti laser ranging and marked target seeking equipment. (*Crown copyright*)

they remained Harriers. They formed a training unit and three operational squadrons, which at times provided detachments in aircraft carriers. The Spanish Navy bought 11 AV-8As and two TAV-8As for operations from the carrier *Dédalo*, although the purchase was made via the US Navy (which service had bought AV-8As on behalf of the USMC) in order to avoid the stigma of dealing directly with the nation that still held on to Gibraltar.

In 1972 HSA was awarded a contract to study the possibility of developing a carrier-based version of the Harrier, primarily to provide air defence against low speed maritime patrol aircraft for the RN's anti-submarine carriers, a role that land-based aircraft were failing to provide. Various sea trials had been carried out with P.1127s and Harriers, and the USMC was to base AV-8As on carriers for much longer periods, but the Harrier had several components that corroded fairly easily, and its operational equipment was never intended for carrier operations and the air defence role.

In 1975, thanks largely to pressure from trades unions on the British Government, supported by some highly optimistic export sales predictions from the company, the intention to acquire Sea Harriers was formally announced by MOD. However, once again it was to be a minimum change programme. Magnesium was to be deleted wherever possible, a nose radar was to be added, the reaction controls improved, and the inertial navigation system was to be replaced by a Doppler-TGP combination that avoided the problem of alignment on deck. Fortunately, the nose radar provided an excuse to redesign the front fuselage, giving a much better cockpit and a worthwhile rear view. On the other hand the radar (Ferranti Blue Fox) was to be a straightforward derivative of the Sea Spray used in the Westland Lynx helicopter, and the air defence armament was restricted to two 30 mm Aden cannon (i.e., half the armament of the old Hunter) and two AIM-9 Sidewinders.

Being intended to destroy medium-level shadowing aircraft, the Sea Harrier had no look-down capability over land and only a limited capability over water. Whether its armament was really good enough to dispatch at Tu-95 *Bear* fitted with chaff/flare dispensers has never been established. The only large aircraft to have been shot down by a Sea Harrier was an Argentine C-130, which took one Sidewinder in the wing (the other having fallen short) and all 200 rounds of 30 mm, which were believed to have damaged the flying controls, since the aircraft then spiralled down into the sea.

The Sea Harrier benefited from the use of a ski-jump deck, made possible by the fact that (unlike the Indian Navy, for example) the RN had no interest in operating CTOL aircraft from the ship. The merits of the ski-jump concept were made clear by a study of the effect of deck pitching on take-off performance: it was evident that higher weights could be used if the deck was given a permanent upward bias. In essence, the ski-jump resulted in the aircraft leaving the deck with an upward velocity component, though well below the speed at which its weight could be equalled by the combination of jet lift and wing lift. This vertical speed component gave the aircraft time to accelerate to a speed at which it could support its own weight. In principle, the use of a ski-jump was no different from the pioneering aviator aiming for the biggest bump in the airfield, when piloting a flying machine with barely sufficient power for a conventional take-off.

Unfortunately, there was nothing analogous to the ski-jump when it came to landing. Thrust development of the Pegasus had been terminated when production engines reached 21,500 lb (9,750 kg) in 1971. As aircraft weight edged upwards due to modifications, vertical landings became marginal, especially for the high temperatures encountered by the Indian Navy, which bought Sea Harriers and some two-seaters with most of the operational equipment of the naval version (aside from the radar). An initial update for the RN aircraft introduced the BAe Sea Eagle sea-skimming anti-ship missile, and the mid-life update will replace the Blue Fox radar with the much improved Blue Vixen, which will have a look-down capability and will be compatible with the AMRAAM missile. Vertical landings with missiles in place clearly require some thrust increase.

In view of its vastly improved cockpit, the Sea Harrier was taken as the basis for later export proposals, including variants for land-based operations without radar. Both land-based and sea-based versions were offered to China.

Why Didn't It Sell?

From 1967 onwards Kingston had a strong marketing team, tasked with selling the Harrier in all overseas countries except for the US and those places for which export licences would not have

been granted (broadly speaking, the Communist Bloc, Chile and South Africa). The fact that the team succeeded in only two countries (Spain and India) has naturally been a bitter disappointment, making nonsense of all the optimistic forecasts. At one point in the 1970s the Harrier had been sold to the US and Spain, and appeared to be on the point of a massive breakthrough in China, a third country that had been dismissed as a 'hopeless' sales prospect in the initial predictions. The obvious implication was that marketing efforts should be concentrated on South Africa, Chile and France!

Why Harrier marketing has failed so abysmally remains a matter of opinion. In this writer's view, we were trying to sell (without the official support we really needed) a highly innovative product that was extremely expensive, yet which sacrificed the supersonic performance that everyone wanted, while achieving an airfield performance that only a small percentage of the world's air forces actually required.

The sheer innovation of V/STOL was a strong disincentive to purchases, as long as the aircraft lacked an impeccable endorsement from a major operator. Even the RAF's support was half-hearted: the service bought 151 Harriers and 201 CTOL Jaguars. If the USAF had accepted the Harrier, far more aircraft might well have been sold elsewhere, but the USMC purchase apparently influenced no-one except the Spanish Navy. The Marines simply were not representative of any other air force; as a service obsessed with amphibious landings they were unique.

It is also arguable that the innovation of V/STOL needed to be counterbalanced by high level political support, which was absent. Whereas France's head of state (i.e., the President) can play a direct role in arms sales, Britain's Queen can play only an indirect part. This situation places a much greater responsibility on the Prime Minister, yet prior to Margaret Thatcher no British PM took an active interest in defence equipment sales. By the same token, in the early days of Harrier marketing very few British military attachés felt it their duty to be involved in arms exports.

The most important single technical factor militating against

The most affordable of supersonic fighters, the Northrop F-5A (illustrated here by RNethAF NF-5As) kept less wealthy Western air forces in business until better equipment came along.

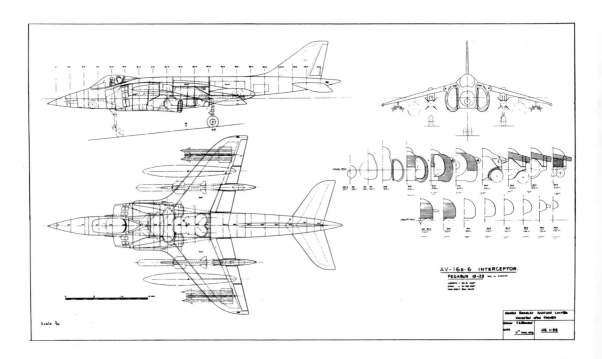

AV-16s-6 INTERCEPTOR.
PEGASUS 15-23

TOP LEFT In the early 1970s HSA proposed a supersonic Harrier derivative named the AV-16, which had a Pegasus 15 with PCB and drooped nozzles. This was one of a series of joint efforts with MDC. (*BAe*)

LEFT This Pakistan Air Force Mirage 5 exemplifies the marketing success of the Dassault-Breguet Mirage III/5 series. Like the preceding Hawker Hunter, this was a moderately-priced, multi-role aircraft.

ABOVE Intended as a STOL soft-field aircraft that would provide a large-scale workload for Italian industry, the Fiat G.91R was a small, low-cost aircraft that sold in large numbers. (*Fiat*)

Harrier purchases was its lack of supersonic capability, which most operators expected to find in such an expensive aircraft. Many also expressed surprise that a modern aircraft should have no radar. In vain Harrier salesmen insisted that few aircraft were capable of exceeding Mach 1.0 at sea level, and then only for a few minutes at a time, with horrendous fuel flows. Most air forces wanted to be able to fly a HI-LO mission, and they felt that at altitude it would be a dead duck.

There was also a feeling that the V/STOL concept had been ruled invalid by the switch from planning on an all-out war to a graduated response, with several days of conventional warfare. In addition, both France and Germany had looked very seriously at V/STOL and had chosen instead the 'fortress airfield' concept. It is also true that dispersal is not applicable in all countries: it needs a good road network, natural camouflage, and security on the ground. In some respects Germany is a natural for V/STOL, although there have always been doubts about the threat from Spetsnaz teams.

It may be instructive to consider a few individual cases. The USAF refused to take a serious interest in the Harrier (although the service funded the NASA trials of P.1127 models) because at the time the combination of Mach 2 dash and 2,000 nm (3,700 km) ferry range was considered essential in future combat aircraft. As stated above, Germany had made a policy decision against V/STOL, and in any event was intent on having two engines (following the F-104G accidents) and on buying from the US to offset the cost of American troops being stationed in Europe. At one stage the French Navy showed an interest in the Sea Harrier, though it was clear that it would have to be built by Dassault-Breguet, or traded for a French aircraft. Sweden was an obvious potential customer, since the Harrier was fully compatible with SAF dispersal concepts, but it would have meant the RAF having the AJ.37 Viggen in place of the Buccaneer. China was a serious possibility in view of the threat to its airfields, though some operating areas along the Soviet border are quite high for V/STOL operations. However, the purchase and licence arrangements were delayed for many months by the British Government. By the time that approval finally came, the Chinese were short of hard currency, and what would have been a very large deal fell through.

It may also be noted that the Harrier was basically unsuited to many Third World air forces. Few really faced a serious threat of runway bombing. Few needed the sophistication or the maintenance demands of the Harrier nav-attack system, yet it was very late in the programme that overseas buyers were offered the much simpler USMC fit.

Some operators undoubtedly felt that a Harrier purchase would have made nonsense of the CTOL aircraft that made up the rest of their fleets. The argument that it was perfectly rational to have a V/STOL component as an insurance policy was not accepted, although this is presumably how the RAF justifies its support for the Harrier.

The Sea Harrier is a basically more saleable product, though even more expensive. Whereas land-based V/STOL pays off only in war, naval V/STOL saves money in peacetime, since Sea Harriers can be operated from far less expensive ships than comparable CTOL aircraft such as the Dassault-Breguet Super Etendard. The Spanish Navy bought the AV-8A because at the time there was a need to provide air defence for convoys operating between Spain and what was then the Spanish Sahara. The Indian Navy bought the Sea Harrier because it intended to build up a three-carrier force, and this was the affordable way to do it. (The Yak-38 was not offered on a similar timescale). However, the number of navies with fixed-wing ambitions is severely limited, and two prospects were eliminated by the 1982 war in the South Atlantic.

Second Generation

In 1969 HSA signed an agreement with McDonnell Douglas, giving the American company licence-production rights for the Harrier/AV-8A and providing for the exchange of information on

Italy's principal V/STOL project was the Fiat G.95/4, which was to have had four lift engines in the centre fuselage. (Fiat)

ABOVE A model of Kingston's proposed Advanced Harrier, the so-called 'GR.5(K)'. (*BAe*)

TOP RIGHT The McDonnell Douglas AV-8B at the hover, showing its raised cockpit, large strakes and new nose shape. The pitot-static nose probe suggests that this was a development aircraft. (*MDC*)

RIGHT A production AV-8B for the USMC, with TER-laden bombs. Note the inset outriggers, to simplify operations from roads and manoeuvring on packed carrier decks. (*MDC*)

Harrier-derived future projects. In the event, licence construction in the US was not required, but the agreement initiated long-term collaboration between the two organizations. This cooperation included joint studies in the early 1970s of the AV-16, designed around the Pegasus 15 of 24,500 lb (11,110 kg) thrust and an enlarged supercritical wing. The AV-16 was proposed in both subsonic and supersonic forms (the latter with PCB) for the USMC, USN, RAF and RN, but in the end there was not sufficient common ground between the four services, and the Pegasus 15 was too expensive, so the programme was terminated.

Following the AV-16, the two companies pursued independent lines, each studying big-wing Harrier derivatives with the existing engine of 21,500 lb (9,750 kg). In 1975 Kingston was awarded a MOD research contract to design an advanced wing that could be retrofitted to RAF Harriers, primarily to improve the aircraft's self-defence capability by increasing manoeuvrability and providing two extra pylons for Sidewinders. At the same time internal fuel volume was to be increased, STO performance was to be improved, and the outrigger track was to be reduced to facilitate operations from narrow road surfaces. It may be noted that the AV-8B wing was unsuitable for retrofit, because the supercritical section took the centre of pressure further aft, increasing downloads on the tail and associated stress levels in the rear fuselage.

Compared to the standard 201 sq ft (18.7 m^2) Harrier wing, the new design was 25 per cent larger, at 250 sq ft (23.2 m^2), and the span was increased to take the aspect ratio from 3.2 to 4.1. Leading edge sweep was reduced from 40.4 to 37.5 degrees. Instead of tapering from 10.1 to 3.9 per cent in thickness/chord ratio, the new wing went from 12.5 to 9.2, giving far more fuel volume. Outrigger track was reduced from 22.2 to 18.0 ft (6.77 to 5.49 m), and two pylons were added. The wing was fitted with leading edge root extensions (LERX) and single-slot flaps.

The 'Advanced Harrier' proposed to MOD in 1979 combined this big wing with 40 per cent more fuel volume, a Sea Harrier front fuselage, air intakes similar to those of the AV-8B, and an uprated engine giving around 23,000 lb (10,430 kg) thrust.

However, technically the most interesting innovation proposed was the use of thrust reversal for short landings at high weights, using 160 degrees of nozzle rotation instead of the Harrier's normal 98 degrees. The driving force behind this move was that the aircraft was almost 1,200 lb (545 kg) heavier than the standard Harrier, which was marginal in vertical landing performance.

From the outset of the P.1127 programme, development has been restricted to vertical and short take-off (the latter being the normal mode), but only vertical landings, hence the widely used term STOVL. However, the possibility of using short landings at high weights has always been present in principle. The short landing mode has been neglected not because of any insuperable problem, but because pilots like the ability to stop and land, rather than landing and then trying to stop. The only serious considerations against thrust reversal are possible debris ingestion and the problem of holding the aircraft straight while blowing up clouds of steam from a wet surface, but these matters are not regarded as insuperable.

Kingston had high hopes that the RAF would accept the Advanced Harrier to replace the GR.3, but the AV-8B was chosen in its place. The McDonnell Douglas aircraft differs basically in having a lightweight carbon fibre wing with a supercritical section, and in lacking the thrust reversal provisions of the British proposal. Wing area was set at a nominal 230 sq ft (21.4 m^2), increasing internal fuel volume from the original 5,056 lb (2,293 kg) to 7,759 lb (3,520 kg). The use of advanced composite materials is estimated to have saved around 300 lb (150 kg) relative to a metal wing of the same size. Carbon fibre is also used in many other components, including the new front fuselage. The front nozzles are extended and sawn off at right angles, giving a slight increase in static thrust, although the emphasis in engine development has been to improve reliability and time between component overhauls, rather than to increase thrust. The AV-8B is fitted with small LERX (the result of British research), and more advanced LIDS (lift-improvement devices), combining enlarged strakes and a retractable cross-dam.

The British version (Harrier GR.5/7) differs only in regard to some items of equipment, including Martin-Baker seats instead of Stencels, and two Aden-25 cannon in place of the GE GAU-12/U five-barrel 25 mm. The operators will undoubtedly find the AV-8B a vast improvement over the Harrier/AV-8A, giving for a fixed take-off distance roughly twice the warload or radius of action. The AV-8B also has far better V/STOL handling than the first

The first Harrier GR.5 for the RAF. The first few GR.5s were initially painted a countershaded grey, which was good in terms of air-air visibility, but was too easily seen on the ground. All later aircraft were painted green. (*BAe*)

The first RAF Harrier GR.5 in flight. Unlike the basic AV-8B, the GR.5 has two weapon stations for AIM-9s ahead of the outriggers. (*BAe*)

Cutaway view of the AV-8B, the dark areas in the wing and alongside and behind the engine indicating fuel tanks. (*BAe*)

A Marine Corps AV-8B
loaded with retarded
bombs. (*MDC*)

The square-nozzle Rolls-
Royce Pegasus F402 for
the AV-8B. (*R-R*)

generation. However, it is a great shame that HSA and MDC did not work together in the initial development of the aircraft, combining the American company's know-how in the field of composite materials with British know-how in the aerodynamic development of moderately swept wings for the ground attack role.

Since the original catastrophically unsuccessful cropped-delta wing of the prototype P.1127, HSA had learned a great deal about the design of moderately swept wings for use at high subsonic speeds. It is quite possible that the AV-8B would have been a faster aeroplane if it had employed the shape of wing proposed by HSA for the Advanced Harrier. Although it was unlikely that any derivative with a substantially enlarged wing would maintain the 635 knots (1,177 km/hr) of the Harrier GR.3 at sea level, the AV-8B initially encountered a problem with premature drag-rise, restricting speed to a level that some accounts put as low as 462 knots (856 km/hr)! There followed a drag-reduction programme and an engine modification to increase combat rating, leading to a sea level speed that is now quoted as 562 knots (1,040 km/hr). This figure is less than remarkable, but it is a speed that the USMC and RAF can live with.

By late 1989 improved AV-8Bs and Harrier GR.7s are scheduled to be operational with a head-up presentation of a FLIR picture, supplemented by night vision goggles to permit low level operations at night. A radar-equipped version has also been proposed. As a result of the RAF order, British Aerospace will perform 40 per cent of the airframe work on the combined USMC and RAF orders, and 25 per cent in the case of other orders, such as that for Spain. Rolls-Royce is building all the Pegasus engines, although Pratt & Whitney may manufacture up to 25 per cent by value of the engines for the US forces. From 1990 AV-8Bs will be delivered with the Pegasus II-61 (F402-RR-408), giving twice the life and a thrust increase of 3,000 lb (1,360 kg).

6

Operational Experience of V/STOL

This sequence of photographs illustrates dispersal exercises with Harriers of RAF Germany, using woods and camouflage nets for cover, but operating from adjacent roads. In wartime, urban dispersal would also be used, but for obvious reasons this concept cannot be tested in peacetime. (*Crown copyright/RAF Germany*)

Early flight trials with the P.1127 demonstrated the technical feasibility of V/STOL, but the basic idea of dispersing aircraft to small sites runs counter to traditional air force doctrine, which states that distributing air assets in 'penny packages' is fundamentally wasteful (and what would happen if ever the army won back control of fixed wing aircraft). Air forces are accustomed to operating as large units from fixed bases, and there was initially some concern that dispersed operation would involve not only difficulties with servicing, repairs, logistics and communications, but also considerable additional costs due to the need for extra manpower, vehicles and ground support equipment, and due to the general inefficiency of small-scale operating units. In the event, both the principal Harrier operators quite clearly regard their experience with the Harrier as having validated the advantages claimed for V/STOL, although both services welcome the warload-radius enhancement and the improvement in handling provided by the second Harrier generation.

Harriers With RAF Germany

In principle RAF Harriers can be deployed anywhere in the world, as instanced by the detachment at Belize, where these aircraft have been stationed since 1975 (Harriers being used primarily because Guatemalan forces could fairly easily put the runway out of action). However, the main purpose of RAF Harriers is to oppose a Soviet armoured thrust on the Central Front, hence the real test of the feasibility of v/STOL is in Germany.

At time of writing 36 Harrier GR.3s equip two large squadrons based at Gütersloh, near the East German border. Their role in war would be to attack armoured vehicles of the Warsaw Pact second echelon and reserve forces up to 55 nm (100 km) behind the front line. It is envisaged that they would be employed in mass attacks in combination with other NATO ground attack aircraft against concentrations of armour, such as a tank column crossing a river. They would also be used in tactical reconnaissance and anti-helicopter duties.

At Gütersloh the Harriers are normally protected in reinforced concrete hangars, which were originally built to house Lightnings. The base is defended by the Rapier SAMs of the RAF Regiment's No 63 Sqn. During the build-up to war, the Harriers would be dispersed forward to pre-selected sites, to avoid the possibility of them being wiped out at the main base by a surprise nuclear attack. British plans are based on the belief that there would be several days of warning signs, such as the forward movement of Warsaw Pact forces, the deployment of naval forces from bases around the Kola Peninsula, and the clearing of routes through minefields adjacent to the border to allow their armour to attack.

From peacetime exercises it is anticipated that the dispersal sites would probably be located in the Teutoburger Wald, although they could also be around Gütersloh. The 36 aircraft would be divided between six forward sites, each trio of operating sites being grouped around a logistics park. For each of the two squadrons there would be a primary site, commanded by the squadron commander, and two sub-sites run by flight commanders. It seems likely that the sites would either have been used previously in training exercises, or selected for the availability of hard operating surfaces and suitable cover (woods, barns or disused farmhouses). Once war was declared, the options would be increased, since urban dispersal could be employed, with sites based on commandeered buildings on the outskirts of towns. Each site would have basic servicing and repair facilites, plus fuel and weapons for at least two days of operations, since resupply by road could easily be restricted by the flood of refugees. It has been claimed that a Harrier can fly eight 30-minute sorties in the course

of a day, assuming a 30-minute turnround and that it remains serviceable. The two squadrons together are expected to generate over 200 sorties per day. It is planned that pilots would fly two or three sorties in sequence, totalling perhaps five or six sorties per pilot per day.

The idea of the two squadrons generating over 200 sorties per day does not appear to have been demonstrated by peacetime trials, but the RAF seems to be confident that the pressures and relaxed procedures of a real war would enable this figure to be achieved. In Exercise Oak Stroll in West Germany in 1974, the RAF began with 28 serviceable Harriers, and generated 1,120 sorties over the course of nine days, corresponding to 124 sorties per day, and 4.4 sorties per day per initial aircraft. In a real war, it is quite possible that the strength of the wing would have been brought up to 36 aircraft by reinforcement from the OCU, which on this basis would have generated 160 sorties per day. It is also worth noting that in Exercise Big Tee in England in 1974 an initial force of 12 Harriers generated more than 360 sorties over three days, corresponding to more than 10 sorties per day per initial aircraft. The manufacturer points out that during the Falklands conflict of 1982 Harrier availability was maintained at over 95 per cent despite appalling conditions, and that only one per cent of planned missions were cancelled due to unserviceability.

Site security would be the responsibility of two squadrons of the RAF Regiment. Originally these units were broadly equivalent to an infantry company, each squadron having around 120 men, though they had somewhat more firepower in the form of 81 mm mortars, Carl Gustav anti-tank rocket launchers, and GPMGS. However, as field squadrons their mobility depended on Land Rovers and 4-ton trucks. More recently they have become light armoured squadrons, each with six Scorpion light tanks with 76 mm guns, 15 Spartan APCs, one Sultan command post vehicle, and a Samson armoured recovery vehicle. In addition to these vehicles in the Alvis CVR(T) range, they each retain 11 Land Rovers and one 4-ton truck.

Harrier squadron personnel are trained in combat and could provide some assistance to the RAF Regiment. However, security would largely depend on concealment, and on the ability to relocate the site if necessary. The sites and logistics parks are difficult to find from the air. They can be found with IR photography, but it is felt that the Soviets would not find it cost-effective to use large numbers of aircraft in intense search efforts, especially as the sites can be moved quite quickly. Site relocation is practised regularly in peacetime, the alternative sites being preselected to minimize organizational problems. Reports indicate that a site may be vacated with all essential equipment within one hour, and that the alternative may be operational within two or three hours. This assumes a typical move of less than 10 miles (16 km). The logistics park is naturally less mobile, but on the other hand its location is not likely to be disclosed by aircraft movements—noisily obvious to any enemy agent in the vicinity.

Communications benefit from the use of secure British Army facilities, with the two primary sites linked directly to the Air Support Operations Centres (ASOCs) with the 1st British Corps and the two flanking corps of NORTHAG. All the sites are linked via secure communications, not only to the Harrier Force HQ (which is housed in trailers protected against NBC attack) but also among themselves. Pilots may be tasked via a telebrief facility while in the cockpit.

Although dispersed operations are somewhat more difficult in peacetime than those from a conventional airfield, Harrier squadrons have consistently received very high marks in NATO TACEVALS (tactical evaluations), which provide independent assessments of alert posture, mission effectiveness, support functions, and the ability to survive air and land attacks. It has been reported that MOD estimates that it costs 10 to 15 per cent more to operate a Harrier unit from dispersed sites, rather than from a main base. However, it has also been suggested that if the full costs of main base operation were taken into account, including hardened shelters and air defence systems, then there would probably be no difference between the two operational concepts. In any event, the cost premium of dispersal is certainly small, and easily justified in terms of the V/STOL aircraft's ability to survive any conceivable level of air attack.

A report written in 1981 stated that dispersal to six sites would involve the use of around 400 vehicles out of the 600 or more employed in support of the Harrier force in Germany, and some 440 maintenance personnel out of the 560 technicians at Gütersloh. All essential servicing and maintenance can be done in the field, including an engine change, for which a special rig has

been developed to allow the engine to be lifted out of the airframe. It has always been a bad feature of the Harrier that an engine change requires the supporting of the fuselage and the removal of the wing, which is time-consuming and disturbs a number of systems, requiring subsequent checks. In the case of the P.1154 and HS.1170 the aircraft would have been jacked up and the engine dropped out, leaving the wing in place.

AV-8s with the US Marine Corps

Whereas the RAF in Germany would use V/STOL to ensure survival (despite any level of conventional or NBC attacks on main bases) through dispersal in small operating units, the USMC would employ V/STOL basically to provide close air support for amphibious landing forces in areas where no conventional airfields exist. Because of its minimal operating site requirements, the Harrier can be moved ashore much more quickly than a CTOL aircraft, and can thus provide a faster reaction capability in response to calls for supporting fire. To achieve the same reaction times, a conventional aircraft has to maintain standing patrols (sometimes described as 'loiter and jettison'), which are expensive and create additional logistic demands.

As the Marines advance inland, larger and better-equipped bases would be established, while the small operating sites would move to stay close to the forward lines. As happened in Vietnam, the Marines may also be required to function virtually as an Army unit, occupying ground and withstanding attacks from both insurgents and conventional ground forces. The USMC concept of operations thus has to be sufficiently flexible to deal with a variety of scenarios, rather than just the traditional amphibious assault.

The Marine concept is based on three categories of ground location, and derives from extensive testing with the AV-8A. The simplest type of base is an austere VTOL forward site, which in a light forest could be built by 19 to 25 men in the course of literally one or two days. If the scenario is such that an existing operating surface such as a road is available, then the time for site construction is a matter of a few hours.

If no surface suitable for STO is available, then a VTOL pad of aluminium planking, 72 ft (22 m) square, would be laid on any reasonably flat surface, and the surrounding area cleared to a distance of 150 ft (45 m) in all directions. Up to four AV-8s would operate from such a site, using a ground (rather than airborne) loiter. The site would be located in a secure area typically 20 nm (37 km) from the forward lines. Initially, it might be necessary (if fuel and ordnance were not available at the site) for the aircraft to be replenished aboard ship, land vertically at the site, and return to the ship after completing each mission. However, as soon as helicopters became available to supply the site, the AV-8s could be rearmed and refuelled there, thus increasing the sortie rate available. It is estimated that three deliveries by the Sikorsky CH-53E Super Stallion could typically provide more than 36 tons of fuel and ordnance, making possible 12 sorties by the AV-8s. The Marines do not envisage carrying out any type of maintenance at these forward sites.

Whereas the forward site would provide sustained daytime VFR operations, the movement of the battle inland would enable the construction of an AV-8 'facility' supporting both day and night VFR operations. The facility is seen as an intermediate-size base, located at around 50 nm (90 km) behind the forward lines. It would have a runway 600 ft (180 m) long and 72 ft (22 m) wide, and would support operations by between six and ten AV-8s. Depending on the terrain and the manpower available, construction of the facility is expected to take 24–72 hours, and to involve the use of around 325 tons of equipment, representing 30 sorties by the CH-53E. Some maintenance facilities would be provided.

In the event that sufficient territory was available, the Marines would construct a main base approximately 100 nm (185 km) from the front lines, with a squardon of 20 AV-8s, and more comprehensive maintenance facilities. The main base would be equipped to provide day/night all-weather operations.

The Marines have found that, aside from providing advantages in close support operations, AV-8s have also demonstrated some useful features in operating from carriers. The AV-8As were first used from LPHS and LPDS as far back as 1971, when the type entered service, but the first CV operation took place in 1976, when VMA-231 was deployed on board the USS *Franklin D Roosevelt* (CV-42) as part of CVW-19, which consisted basically of two F-4 Phantom II and three A-7 Corsair II squadrons.

A number of aspects of AV-8A operation received favourable comment. Compared to the F-4s and A-7s, the AV-8A had the

advantage that it was self-starting, whereas the others required power units to be available. The use of STO reduced delays in launching, since there was no catapult hook-up procedure. In the recovery phase an area of 50 ft (15 m) radius sufficed, increasing the parking area, and there were no wave-offs, since (in the event of any delay) the following aircraft simply hovered until its predecessor had landed. The fact that the arresting system was not required was also seen as a positive improvement. In addition, deck handling was simplified by the aircraft's ability to reverse into the desired position, using the 98 degree nozzle position to provide a rearward thrust component.

Operational advantages included the aircraft's ability to launch and recover when the carrier was steaming at slow speed and with a substantial crosswind component, e.g., in transiting a minefield or narrow straits. The AV-8As could thus defend the carrier against airborne or surface attackers under conditions when neither the F-4 nor the A-7 could be operated. None of the Harrier operations carried out while the carrier was crossing the Atlantic necessitated any change in the ship's course, although on one occasion the wind-over-deck (WOD) was a 15 knot (28 km/hr) tailwind. The AV-8A simply landed heading into wind, which in that instance necessitated approaching over the bow of the ship. Unlike CTOL aircraft, the AV-8A was also able to take off and land while the ship was at anchor, something it could do in spite of the fact that most of the deck was covered with parked aircraft. Aside from providing an air defence capability, this also allowed maintenance checkflights to be performed while the ship was in port.

The flexibility of V/STOL operations was further demonstrated by the aircraft transferring to the USS *Guam* (LPH-9), for which the AV-8As provided an air defence capability under control from the ship. In an amphibious landing exercise, AV-8As also staged from the *Guam* to the USS *Trenton* (LPD-14) for refuelling, using the latter's 196 by 75 ft (60 by 23 m) flight deck.

Although the AV-8A did not replace the functions of the F-4 and A-7, it was found to provide an invaluable additional combat capability, primarily because the carrier could launch and recover at any time (rather than being rigidly limited to cycle times) and could steam on whatever heading was required from tactical considerations.

Helicopter support for dispersed Harrier operations would require large aircraft such as this Sikorsky CH-53E Super Stallion, which can accept payloads of up to 15 tons. (*Sikorsky*)

The first landing by a high performance V/STOL aircraft (the first P.1127, XP831) was carried out by HSA chief test pilot 'Bill' Bedford on 8 February 1963 on HMS *Ark Royal* off Lyme Bay near Portland. Bedford is shown here being greeted by the ship's captain. (*BAe*)

Shipboard trials with the Harrier family included this operation in June 1966 from the 27,300-ton HMS *Bulwark*, a commando carrier. Judging by its 'poor-man's streamwise tip', this was probably the third P.1127, serial XP972. (*BAe*)

British Maritime V/STOL Experience

The first Sea Harrier delivery to the RN took place in June 1979, and the first operational unit was formed in April 1980, serving briefly in HMS *Invincible* before transferring to *Hermes*. The Fleet Air Arm found that V/STOL operations are in many respects simpler and safer than those involving conventional aircraft. The CTOL aircraft requires a fully serviceable catapult, the ship heading into wind, and a large wind-over-deck speed if it is to launch at maximum weight. The V/STOL aircraft requires no special equipment, and a much smaller deck handling crew (since there is no catapult engagement). The WOD requirement is also less restrictive than in the case of a CTOL aircraft. The use of a ski-jump (aside from improving take-off weight under flat sea conditions) also has the advantage that take-off performance is less affected by deck pitching, and that it gives an increased safety margin, compared with a conventional catapult launch. If the engine should experience a total loss of thrust as the wheels leave the deck, a CTOL aircraft will hit the sea in approximately 1.5 seconds, whereas a V/STOL aircraft taking off from a ski-jump in a similar emergency would provide 6.5 seconds for the pilot to eject.

A conventional arrested landing requires a very high skill level from the pilot, since the aircraft must be precisely positioned at touchdown and its speed correctly adjusted. Arriving in the region of 135 knots (250 km/hr), a CTOL aircraft has a great deal of kinetic energy and can cause extensive damage if the arrester system is not engaged properly. It also requires a considerable area of deck and fuel reserves to allow for a wave-off in the event that the deck is not cleared. In contrast, with a V/STOL aircraft there are no missed approaches or wave-offs. If a Sea Harrier recovery is delayed, it simply hovers alongside until its landing spot is free. It lands first time, every time. When recovering under severe pitching conditions that would rule out the landing of CTOL aircraft, the Sea Harrier hovers alongside the amidships landing spot until the deck motion temporarily dies down. A CTOL aircraft is obliged to land on the rear of the flight deck, where the pitching movement is much more severe, and is unable to adjust the instant of touchdown to take advantage of variations in ship motion.

The safety that characterizes naval V/STOL operations is dramatized by the Sea Harrier's ability to recover in as little as 130

Will that funny little aeroplane go down the lift and fit in the hangar without a wing-fold? Yes, no problem. (*BAe*)

The P.1127 re-emerges, ready for take-off. To the surprise of certain MoD officials, the P.1127 wasn't brought down by funnel gases, the deck didn't buckle, and nobody was blown overboard. (*BAe*)

The production Harrier GR.1 was tested from the 50,800 ton *Ark Royal* in 1973. Unfortunately, the ability of RAF Harriers to operate from RN ships was not taken seriously until the Falklands conflict, when various modifications had to be introduced in considerable haste. (*BAe*)

ft (40 m) visibility. On one occasion during the 1982 conflict with Argentina, visibility was severely restricted, and the aircraft approached the carrier with assistance from flares thrown over the stern. With guidance from controllers on the ship, the Sea Harrier was brought to the hover at a height of 65 ft (20 m) alongside the ship. The pilot then translated the aircraft sideways until it was seen from the flying control position on the bridge. He was then guided to a position where he could see the landing spot and completed the recovery visually.

The operational flexibility of the Sea Harrier was demonstrated in the *Alraigo* incident of June 1983, when an inexperienced Sub-Lieutenant, flying from HMS *Illustrious*, experienced a navigation system failure and landed on the 2,300 ton Spanish freighter. The pilot set the aircraft down on containers on the deck, then retracted the undercarriage to restrict movement. The Sea Harrier was lifted off by crane when the ship reached port, and required only minor repairs before it was flying again. Had it been a conventional aircraft, it would have been lost.

To summarize peacetime experience, since the first P.1127 naval trials from HMS *Ark Royal* in 1963 the Harrier series has operated from a wide range of ship types from 80,000 ton US Navy attack carriers down to vessels of less than 7,000 tons. Aside from carrier decks, Harriers have also used the helicopter platforms on the rear of smaller ships such as the 12,500 ton cruiser *Blake*. In the 1969 Harrier trials from *Blake*, the helicopter platform was rolling through 10 degrees, with a 35 knot (65 km/hr) WOD. The broad conclusions were that V/STOL offered a range of advantages, while posing none of the problems that had been feared. Metal flight decks did not buckle, and the wooden flight deck of the *Dédalo* did not catch fire, since the hot gases could be pointed aft during engine checks and as soon as the aircraft had touched down. There were no cliff-edge effects as the aircraft crossed the limits of the deck. Turbulence effects from the superstructure and hot gas ingestion from the funnel were minor considerations, and easily avoided.

Harriers At War

For 13 years from the date of the Harrier's introduction into service in April 1969 the aircraft was not operated in anger. There had been exercises, in which the practicality of dispersed

First of the RN's new carriers, *Invincible* has a small skijump at the bow, restricted in size by the Sea Dart launcher. The ramp (as in the case of *Illustrious*) is 90 ft (27.4 m) long, with an inclination of 7 degrees. (HMS *Invincible*)

operation in Germany had received full marks, and in which Sea Harriers had provided a useful air defence capability for NATO naval units, supported by US Navy Grumman E-2C airborne early warning (AEW) aircraft. In simulated close combats Sea Harriers had performed astonishingly well against the latest supersonic US fighters, so well that the Fleet Air Arm had to ask journalists not to publish the kill-ratios achieved, to avoid embarrassment to the USAF and USN.

Nonetheless, in the eyes of many observers the Harrier family was merely a PR exercise to show that Britain still led the world in some branch of aviation. In reality (they believed) its warload-radius performance in the ground attack role was negligible. In air defence, it would be massacred as soon as it climbed to heights at which other aircraft could use their supersonic capability. Harrier salesmen swore that it would prove its value in any war, but very few operators believed them.

An Israeli-built Dagger of the *VIth Brigada Aérea*, photographed at its peacetime base at Tandil. Daggers were operated from the airfields at Rio Gallegos and Rio Grande. (*Michael O'Leary*)

Then in the course of six week of 1982 the interesting theories were overtaken by facts. The aeroplane that was going to be massacred in the air defence role somehow managed to shoot down 23 enemy aircraft (including Mach 2 Mirages and Daggers) without a single loss in air combat. The aeroplane that could carry 'a cigarette packet for the length of a cricket pitch' somehow

Two Sidewinder-armed Sea Harriers about to land. Although intended primarily to defend convoys against the threat of large, low-speed maritime patrol aircraft, the Sea Harrier performed well in the South Atlantic against high performance attack aircraft and fighters. (HMS *Invincible*)

HMS *Hermes*, **which was subsequently sold to the Indian Navy, served as the flagship for the Falklands task force. Note the much larger (12 degree) skijump, restricted in size primarily by the captain's forward view.** (*R-N*)

HMS *Invincible*, **with two Sea Harriers about to launch themselves down the 'tramlines' painted on the deck.** (HMS *Invincible*)

transformed an enemy airbase into a moonscape of bomb craters. The conflict in the South Atlantic ended a great deal of ill-informed criticism of the Harrier family, and it also provided a very striking demonstration of the operational flexibility of the series.

The invasion of the Falklands by Argentine forces took place in the early hours of April 2nd. At that stage the two RN Sea Harrier operational squadrons had 12 aircraft between them, while the training unit had a further eight. In addition, four were being used for various trials, and seven were in storage. It says a great deal for the aircraft and for Navy engineers that 20 Sea Harriers sailed for the South Atlantic with the carrier battle group on April 5th, and that eight more left within a week.

Argentina was estimated to have between 120 and 200 combat aircraft, giving initially a numerical advantage of better than 6:1. The Argentines had four major airfields within 500 nm (925 km) of the Falklands, hence any amphibious landing would be subjected to intense air opposition. In addition, Argentina possessed two KC-130H tankers, which could extend the radius of the A-4s and Super Etendards well beyond the islands, and it was conceivable that either of these types could be operated from the 4,250 ft (1,300 m) runway at Port Stanley. It was thus clear from the outset that any attempt to regain the Falklands by force was doomed to failure, unless some measure of air cover could be provided for the amphibious forces. Thus, if there had been no Sea Harriers, the British Task Force would have lost its credibility, and the Falklands would have remained 'Las Malvinas'.

It was nonetheless obvious that the Argentine numerical advantage of 6:1 or more would make it unlikely that the RN could repeat its peacetime kill-ratios against USAF and USN fighters. It was also clear that a force of 20 Sea Harriers could sustain regular losses for only a short period of time. The MOD estimate was one aircraft lost per day (a figure that was not given to the Sea Harrier squadrons until after the conflict), which threatened to reduce the force to a token strength within two weeks. It was therefore decided to send further Harriers south as reinforcements.

A batch of eight Sea Harriers to follow the original 20 left only three in the UK, with further deliveries from the production line three years away. Since attrition to enemy fire and operational accidents had to be anticipated, and since losses could not be replaced, the decision was taken to augment the Sea Harriers with

A Dassault-Breguet Super Etendard of the French Navy is launched by the waist catapult on the angled deck of the carrier *Foch*, the launch bridle falling into the sea. (*Jean-Pierre Montbazet*)

The CTOL equivalent of the Sea Harrier, this Super Etendard is about to be launched from the *Foch*. (*Jean-Pierre Montbazet*)

RAF Harrier GR.3s. These were to have *ad hoc* modifications to allow the use of Sidewinders in visual air defence duties and to permit their inertial platforms to be aligned on the carrier deck, giving (as a minimum acceptable standard) a reasonably accurate attitude reference on the HUD. There were other modifications concerned with use of the Paveway laser-guided bomb, the Navy's two-inch (5 cm) rocket, improved sealing and drainage to minimize corrosion, the addition of outrigger shackles, the installation of an I-band transponder for bad weather recovery, and a change to the nosewheel steering system.

To restate the basic assumptions of the operation, the liberation of the Falklands by means of an amphibious assault depended on having air cover against attacks which might come from Argentine bases, from the airfield at Port Stanley, or possibly from the Argentine carrier *Veinticinco de Mayo* (May 25th). That air cover depended in the first instance on the availability of the Sea Harrier, and subsequently on the ability of RAF Harriers to supplement and replace Sea Harriers. This meant not only that the RAF aircraft should be able to operate from what were primarily anti-submarine carriers, but also that RAF pilots had to be able to convert quickly to maritime operation.

In the event, RAF Harriers were able to fly from the two carriers, although the technical problems would have been far less serious if Whitehall planners had forseen the possibility of having to level and align the inertial platform on a moving deck. The point to be emphasized is that the operational problems had no connection with V/STOL. They were concerned with nav-attack systems that needed a fixed base (or information on how that base was moving), the ability to employ Navy weapons, and freedom from salt water corrosion. If anyone in MOD had forseen the need to operate RAF Harriers from ships, the various modifications and special provisions could have been actioned in peacetime, and the whole operation would have gone more smoothly.

Despite the problems that arose due to the shortsightedness in Whitehall, when the need to operate RAF Harriers from RN carriers eventuated, that need was fulfilled at extremely short notice and with considerable success. There is no way that French Air Force Mirages could have been operated from the French Navy's *Clemenceau*-class carriers, or USAF F-15s or F-16s could have flown from even the 90,000 ton *Nimitz*-class. Britain was the only nation

The sheer size of a conventional carrier is exemplified by the 89,600 ton nuclear-powered *Enterprise*, which has an overall length of 1123 ft (342 m) and a maximum beam of 248 ft (76 m). Basically a *Kitty Hawk* class hull modified to provide a prototype for the *Nimitz* class, the *Enterprise* was commissioned in 1961. (*Tony Holmes*)

With hook lowered and airbrakes out, the Super Etendard comes in at over 100 knots for an arrested landing, a considerably more violent experience than the vertical touchdown of the Sea Harrier. (*Jean-Pierre Montbazet*)

in the world with this inter-service operational flexibility, and it was made possible by V/STOL.

The other factor in the equation was ease of pilot conversion. The original plan was that each RAF pilot chosen to operate Harriers in Operation Corporate would make three ski-jump take-offs at RNAS Yeovilton, prior to leaving for the South Atlantic. However, it was quickly decided that there was nothing much to ski-jump take-offs, so the training was reduced to a single flight. The initial six Harrier GR.3s transferred to *Hermes* between May 18th and 20th, and they flew their first operational mission on the 20th, attacking a fuel storage depot with spectacular results.

The unique merits of V/STOL were demonstrated before these aircraft ever went to war, in the way in which they were transported to the South Atlantic. The original plan had been to take the GR.3s south on the container ship *Atlantic Conveyor*, which sailed from Liverpool on April 23rd. However, various delays made this impossible, so the eight GR.3s and eight Sea Harriers were ferried to Ascension Island, a distance of 3,670 nm (6,760 km), which required flight refuelling. The Sea Harrier has a smaller liquid oxygen (LOX) container and had to make one stop in Africa for this to be replenished, but the GR.3s were scheduled to fly straight through, in a time of up to 9 hr 15 min. Two GR.3s were left at Ascension to provide air defence against a possible Argentine Entebbe-style raid, while six GR.3s and eight Sea Harriers were transferred to the *Atlantic Conveyor* by VTOL.

The ship had been provided with an 80 by 50 ft (25 by 15 m) VTOL pad of aluminium planking on the forward deck, and containers stacked three-high on either side of the deck to reduce salt water damage. After landing, each aircraft was moved aft to the parking area by means of a tractor, given a thorough servicing check, and then cocooned in plastic bags to protect it against the elements. The final Sea Harrier to land was not cocooned, but was left on the foredeck armed with Sidewinder missiles, in case the ship should be attacked or shadowed by long-range Argentine aircraft. As it happened, no such problem arose, and the 14 aircraft were duly transferred to the two carriers by VTOL. No other Western combat aircraft could have been taken to war in this way. Two further GR.3s were later ferried directly from Ascension to *Hermes*, and four more were shipped south in the *Contender Bezant*, but arrived too late to take part in actual operations.

Conventional take-off operations from the CVN-65 *Enterprise* are illustrated by this US Navy EA-6B Prowler, one of several types that the service planned in the 1970s to replace with V/STOL aircraft. (*Tony Holmes*)

Once in place on *Hermes* and *Invincible*, the Harriers and Sea Harriers functioned in a similar way to CTOL aircraft, although the easing of restrictions on ship heading and WOD enabled the carriers to perform ASW manoeuvres while launching and recovering aircraft. Sea Harriers performed efficiently in the air superiority role on May 1st, when the air battle commenced and the Argentines attempted to win control of the air, so that they could attack the Task Force unhindered. Believing that with a 3.5:1 numerical advantage Mirages and Daggers must prevail against the subsonic Sea Harriers, the Argentine Air Force flew 56 sorties on that first day. When the losses had been counted and the damaged aircraft taken away for repair, it was decided to stop using Mirages and Daggers in the fighter role. Henceforth they were to carry bombs and rely on their superior speed to evade the

Sea Harriers, although many were still lost.

It may be noted that VIFFing was never used in the Falklands, since Argentine aircraft did not have the opportunity to make rear hemisphere attacks on Harriers or Sea Harriers. It is arguable that the real value of the Sea Harrier was in deterring air attacks on the Task Force, since many Argentine aircraft jettisoned their bombs and turned for home when they saw the standing patrols of 'La Muerta Negra' (The Black Death). The actual percentage of Argentine sorties intercepted was small, due to the absence of AEW aircraft, though this situation was rectified after the conflict by the development and deployment of the AEW Sea King helicopter.

The effects of the lack of AEW facilities were worsened by the fact that the carriers had to be held back 200 nm (370 km) to the east, reducing time on station over the Falklands, and eliminating the possibility of rapid reaction sorties from the carrier deck. The situation improved considerably following the opening of 'HMS Sheathbill', an 850 ft (260 m) aluminium planking runway near San Carlos, where the amphibious landing had taken place a few days earlier. The availability of this strip allowed the Sea Harrier pilot to increase his time over the islands from less than 10 minutes to around 30 minutes. At the end of this time, if the Sea Harrier still had its Sidewinders, it could be refuelled and fly a further 20 minutes in the area before returning to the ship. The strip was also used to allow GR.3s to provide quick reaction close support strikes, and permitted aircraft that were running short of fuel to be topped up. This was probably the shortest airstrip ever used in a war by a jet combat aircraft. On one occasion the MEXE matting was raised by the downwash from a Chinook helicopter, but two Sea Harriers that were about to land simply diverted to the helicopter pads of the assault ships HMS Fearless and Intrepid.

After the end of the fighting, some Harrier GR.3s and Sea Harriers were deployed ashore to provide an air defence element, operating from the short runway at Port Stanley until the runway could be extended to accommodate Phantoms. The CTOL aircraft undoubtedly provided a better air defence capability, but the V/STOL aircraft made an air defence system possible much earlier.

The US Navy version of
the V-22 in an
accelerating transition,
with rotors at an
intermediate angle. Note
the early 'T-tail'
configuration. (*Bell
Helicopter Textron*)

7 Further V/STOL Developments

At time of writing it is almost exactly 30 years since Hawker's Ralph Hooper began work on the P.1127 V/STOL combat aircraft project, based on Bristol Siddeley's vectored-thrust front-fan engine, later productionized as the Pegasus. The resulting Harrier eventually entered service 12 years later as a low-cost (and at the time unwelcome) substitute for the supersonic P.1154. The Marine Corps' AV-8A version followed two years later. The second generation in the form of the McDonnell Douglas AV-8B Harrier II has now entered service with the USMC, providing twice the warload or radius, and much better low speed handling characteristics though with some loss of maximum speed. In 1988 the AV-8B (Harrier GR.5) entered service with the RAF. If V/STOL has finally arrived, one can only say that its coming has been at a truly glacial pace.

Hooper's work in the late 1950s probably rates as some of the most innovative ever carried out by the British aircraft industry, but his assessment of the potential market was sadly in error. He believed that he was creating a new class of aircraft that would be operated from small sites close to the front line, and would thus supplement conventional types. These V/STOL studies began only three years after the Hunter entered service, and the underlying assumption was that air forces would buy a V/STOL close support aircraft without waiting to phase out aircraft such as the Hunter. Unfortunately, air forces do not think in this way, and production of the first V/STOL generation had to wait until the Hunter needed replacing.

Comparative cross-sections of a standard Pegasus and one with PCB, showing the large difference in front nozzle temperatures. (R-R)

In looking ahead to the third (and hopefully supersonic) generation, the same sort of restriction applies. The difference is that in the 1950s a manufacturer could afford to start development with his own money, whereas in the 1980s the funding involved would be far beyond the means of even the largest of the British aerospace companies. Nonetheless, with potential demands for such aircraft arising around the end of the century, it can be argued that it is not too soon to begin laying the technological foundations for an advanced V/STOL project.

More than in the case of CTOL aircraft, the key to successful V/STOL development is the powerplant, hence the West should be maintaining some momentum in vectored-thrust engines, while examining other possible options.

As stated earlier, duct-burning in the cold air of the two front engine nozzles (i.e., PCB) is essential to the development of advanced vectored-thrust engines. Although a PCB engine has never been tested in flight on a Harrier, some ground tests were carried out in 1962–65, supplemented by a second series of trials in 1980, and tests with a Pesasus installed in a Harrier airframe in the mid and late 1980s. In the earlier period full-scale running totalled 650 hours, half of which was represented by combustion rig tests, and the other half was PCB trials on the Pegasus 2 and BS.100 engines.

Rolls-Royce has used a Pegasus 11 standard of its vectored thrust turbofan engine for the current phase of PCB tests at P&EE Shoeburyness. (R-R)

The 1980 trials again used a Pegasus 2, and specific operational aspects, such as the effects of water ingestion, inlet distortion, and cross-lighting were investigated. In the following year PCB was tested in the NGTE high altitude facility, to check stability, handling and ignition.

In October 1983 a third new phase began, with a PCB Pegasus 2A installed in an old Harrier airframe, which was suspended from a gantry. This last test programme, sponsored by MOD, was to determine the response of the engine to various levels of intake temperature distortion caused by hot gas reingestion, and the effectiveness of different methods of reducing reingestion. The tests were also to investigate the effects of the PCB exhaust on various ground surfaces and steel decks.

In 1987 Rolls-Royce began another series of PCB tests, using a modified Pegasus II with variable-area front nozzles similar to those of the RB.199. This new programme involves three stages: initial engine runs on a test-stand, further runs on the

ENGINE CONFIGURATION WITH PCB

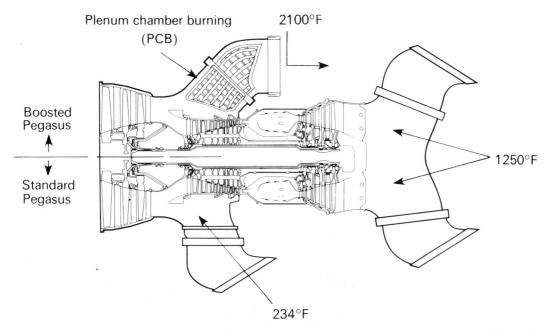

Plenum chamber burning
(PCB)

2100°F

Boosted
Pegasus

Standard
Pegasus

1250°F

234°F

Shoeburyness gantry to allow thrust vectoring, and finally runs with the engine installed in a Harrier airframe. These tests are aimed at measuring and reducing hot gas reingestion, and at measuring PCB nozzle temperature profiles. Other objectives include near-field noise measurement and digital control of PCB fuel scheduling.

Although the powerplant is the critical factor in most respects, there is clearly some advantage if airframe manufacturers continue some project studies to investigate the advantages and disadvantages of different aircraft layouts. For example, although the Harrier series can live with longitudinal instability during transition between jet-borne and wing-borne flight, Kingston designers would prefer to remove the horizontal tail from the downwash field created by partially-deflected jets. One solution would be to use a canard arrangement, but a stable canard is generally held to be limited in maximum lift coefficient due to premature foreplane stall. An alternative approach, which Kingston appears to favour, is to mount the two tailplane halves pointing outboard on widely-separated booms, which also carry the vertical tails.

The twin-boom arrangement also fits in well with the idea of a return to relatively conventional undercarriage configuration, as proposed for many Kingston v/STOL projects in the past. The zero-track tricycle gear of the Harrier is comparatively light, but it leads to outriggers that snap off in heavy landings, and it restricts the length of centreline stores. The alternative is to place conventional main gears in wing-mounted pods, although this incurs a weight penalty due to the length of the legs. It was a small step from wing-mounted maingear pods to booms that also carry the tails, the horizontal members being outboard to avoid the downwash from the jets.

In the early 1980s the Kingston project office produced at least two preliminary designs on the twin-boom theme. The P.1214 'Star Wars' project combined a forward-swept wing (FSW) with an aft-swept tail, but can hardly have been serious, since an FSW needs a foreplane's downwash to avoid root stall. Kingston was much more serious about the P.1216, which was another twin-boom configuration, but with an aft-swept wing.

The still classified P.1216 may well have featured an F-16-style chin intake, which is better suited to high AOA, and suffers less

The PCB combustion system of fuel supply lines and 'colander' flame-holder, based on ramjet experience with the Bloodhound and Sea Dart missiles. (R-R)

No PCB-equipped aircraft has ever flown, but Rolls-Royce ground rig tests have included runs with a PCB Pegasus in a Harrier airframe, suspended from a gantry at Shoeburyness. (R-R)

191

An outdoor PCB test, using a Pegasus with dropped hot nozzles. (R-R)

from birds bouncing off the front fuselage into the inlet. It seems very likely that the twin-boom layout encouraged the use of a three-nozzle engine, to avoid the traditional problem of the front jets pressing the rear (hot) jets against the fuselage sides, with consequent high temperature and fatigue effects.

One of the basic problems of the vectored-thrust concept is that the central location of the engine (which is much further forward than in a conventional design) demands operational equipment in the rear fuselage to balance the weight of the cockpit, pilot, ejection seat, radar, etc in the front. Whether this operational equipment could really be stowed in the twin booms of the P.1216 (to eliminate the need for lead in the tail) is presumably one of the aspects that Kingston investigated. In any event, a full-scale mockup was built, and it was shown to Margaret Thatcher during her visit in December 1982, but the P.1216 has subsequently sunk into oblivion.

BAe Warton's early V/STOL projects included this tilt-engine canard fighter configuration, the P.103. (BAe)

If British Aerospace made no great effort to win funding for the P.1216 as a technology demonstrator, it was probably that Kingston's future was assured by the AV-8B programme and the T-45 version of the Hawk trainer for the US Navy, whereas Warton was facing a desperate future when Tornado production ended around 1989. Warton had to have Government funding for the EAP demonstrator as a lead-in to the Eurofighter, whereas Kingston's situation was less critical. It is nonetheless significant that none of Kingston's engineers had won a place on the BAe main board. When serious work finally begins on the third V/STOL generation, it may well be done at Warton rather than Kingston.

SkyHook

A possible supersonic V/STOL fighter configuration with chin intake and drooped nozzles is tested in model form for hot gas recirculation. Note that the main gear takes the form of two seperate units, mounted on the wings and retracting aft into pods. (BAe)

For several years Kingston has been pressing for MOD support for the 'SkyHook' project, based on the notion that a slightly modified Sea Harrier could be launched and recovered by a relatively small ship equipped with a space-stabilized crane. The basic concept was originated by BAe test pilot Heinz Frick, who was impressed with the ease with which the aircraft could be hovered with great precision. If this hovering accuracy could be combined with a stabilized hook, then the aircraft might be operated from small ships, despite their highly agile decks. Such a development would bring V/STOL aircraft within the reach of far more navies than the relatively conventional ski-jump deck.

A Sea Harrier landing on the VTOL pad of the ill-fated *Atlantic Conveyor* **during the early days of the Falklands conflict.** (HMS *Heron*)

In principle, a crane-mounted hook may be maintained in a straight-line path by placing an inertial platform on the base of the crane, measuring its linear and angular motion, and feeding compensating signals to a fast-acting hydraulic system. The next step would be to give the pilot a special type of display, attached to the crane-head, so that he can place the aircraft in the desired hover position for engagement, which is represented by a cube of 10 ft (3.0 m) sides. One such display system has been tested by BAe, with very satisfactory hover results.

Assuming that the Sea Harrier can be hovered accurately and the crane-head can be stabilized, the third essential is that the 'SkyHook' should be able to engage the aircraft automatically. One such engagement system has been designed (by British Robotic Systems), using an IR sensor on the crane-head and a pattern of IR-absorbing patches on the upper surface of the aircraft. The use of an IR wavelength ensures that the pattern can be illuminated at night without blinding the pilot.

There may well be practical problems, such as the formation of large clouds of spray during low altitude hovers, which would only be found in full-scale trials. However, the real limitation of the 'SkyHook' concept is that the aircraft's start-weight is restricted to that consistent with free-air hover. At the present time the very small disposable load associated with VTO clearly limits the usefulness of the concept for the Harrier/AV-8A generation. It is possible that the AV-8B will offer a slightly more attractive VTO performance, and this will certainly be the case with the third V/STOL generation, although STO will always provide a larger warload and a longer radius. At time of writing there appears to be little prospect of MOD funding trials, or of BAe investing its own money in SkyHook development.

Container Ship Aircraft Carriers

British Aerospace has also been promoting the idea of converting container ships to provide the outer layer of a convoy's air defence system. The conversion includes the installation of a flight deck with a ski-jump, a Plessey surveillance and control radar, six Sea Harriers, two Sea King AEW helicopters, BAe Seawolf point defence missiles, Plessey Shield decoy system, and a Plessey command centre. The concept is referred to as SCADS (Shipboard Containerised Air Defence System).

Once seriously considered by the RAF as a means of providing logistic support for dispersed Harriers in Germany, the Boeing Vertol CH-47C Chinook is shown here carrying a shipping container slung from its underfuselage hook. (*James Hay Stevens*)

The study was based on a ship 700 ft (210 m) long, which was to be fitted with a runway 400 ft (120 m) long and 45 ft (13.7 m) wide, ending in a 12-degree ski-jump. Provisions were to be made for 30 days of operation without replenishment at sea, a crew of 190 men, hangars for two Sea Harriers and one Sea King, and fuel for 50 flight hours per aircraft. The study showed that a total of 233 20 ft (6.1 m) ISO containers would be required. A conversion time of 48 hours was estimated.

The SCADS project might be regarded as an extension of the US Navy Arapaho concept of the late 1960s, under which some container ships would be equipped to operate ASW helicopters in wartime, the conversion kit typically displacing one third of the ship's payload. The concept was tested by the US Navy on the 18,000-ton container ship *Export Leander* in 1982, when pairs of helicopters, including the Sikorsky SH-3H and Boeing-Vertol CH-46 were operated from the two landing spots, each 100 by 64 ft (30 by 20 m). The Arapaho deck is stressed to take heavier helicopters such as the CH-47 Chinook, hence it is more than strong enough for the Harrier series. It is envisaged that an Arapaho-equipped container ship could take up to six Sea Kings (four in the hangar and two on deck) or seven Kaman SH-2Fs, and up to 83,000 Imp gal (380,000 litres) of jet fuel.

The RN subsequently leased this 900-ton installation for trials on the 28,000-ton MV *Astronomer*, which was converted to the

RFA *Reliant* by Cammell Laird. A more comprehensive conversion is being applied to the *Contender Bezant* by Harland & Wolff, though again the emphasis in the first instance is on helicopters rather than Sea Harriers. The resulting aviation training ship, the RFA *Argus*, will be used to train the crews of Sea King, Lynx, and EH-101 helicopters, but in wartime could embark six Sea Kings and 12 Sea Harriers.

Advanced Studies

On 23 January 1986 an MOU was signed by representatives of the US and UK governments, covering joint research over a five-year period into advanced STOVL (ASTOVL) concepts, with reference to the possible development by 1995 of a supersonic fighter technology demonstrator. This collaborative study is to take place in two phases, the first lasting 12–18 months and basically being concerned with comparing four powerplant concepts which might be employed, and the second lasting 3–4 years, and being intended to generate the knowledge from which the shortlisted concepts might be developed. Reports indicate that the study is based on a possible requirement for an air defence fighter employing both subsonic loiter and supersonic dash. The four powerplant concepts being compared in the first stage are:–

(a) vectored-thrust with PCB
(b) remote augmentation lift system (RALS), or 'bleed and burn'
(c) ejector augmentor
(d) tandem fan.

The studies by the engine and airframe manufacturers are being supervised and funded by NASA in the US and MOD in the UK. It is relevant to point out that at time of writing there is no commitment to funding a demonstrator, and that the four basic powerplant concepts are simply options that warrant further work. The end-product could well employ lift engines or it might be a VATOL project, neither of which concepts is listed above, presumably because the basic technology is already understood.

The ejector augmentor scheme was tested many years ago in the Lockheed XV-4B Hummingbird, and was further developed in the case of the Rockwell XFV-12A, which was abandoned before it could be flown. The jet augmentor concept has the potential for producing a low energy downwash, but full-scale thrust

A Rolls-Royce artist's impression of a possible supersonic V/STOL fighter configuration with a three-nozzle vectored-thrust engine. (*R-R*)

augmentation ratios have been disappointing, and it would be surprising to see this idea resurrected.

The tandem-fan concept is almost a return to the original *Gyroptère* proposal, though it is not quite as heavy and complex. For jet-borne operation the efflux from the front fan is diverted downward, and an auxiliary inlet system provides air for the gas generator. Rolls-Royce, having patented the tandem-fan in 1975, also conceived a variation known as the hybrid-fan, in which the efflux from the front fan is discharged at low speeds through rotatable nozzles. The company appears to be keen about the hybrid-fan, but the long shaft connecting the gas generator to the front fan clearly represents a significant weight penalty.

TOP A McDonnell
Douglas study (Model
279-3) of a V/STOL
fighter for the US Navy. It
appears to have a four-
nozzle powerplant, the
front pair being drooped
to avoid pressing the rear
jets against the fuselage.
(*MDC*)

ABOVE Full power for the
Rolls-Royce Pegasus 11
engine with PCB at
Shoeburyness. (*R-R*)

In this writer's view, the two ASTOVL concepts most likely to find
support are the vectored-thrust engine and RALS. This latter
system involves ducting the bypass flow forwards to a remote
combustion system, then exhausting it downwards to provide jet
lift. Once again, it is closely related to an idea promoted by Rolls-
Royce in the 1960s, a concept that had the support of the late Sir
Sydney Camm as a basis for project studies.

It is understood that General Electric has been funded to study
the modification of the 27,600 lb (12,500 kg) F110 afterburning
engine to suit either the RALS or the ejector-augmentor schemes,
although this work is currently outside the US/UK ASTOVL
programme. In parallel with the GE modification, Pratt & Whitney

One of the four advanced
V/STOL engine concepts
being studied under the
joint UK-US programme,
the vectored-thrust
powerplant is shown here
in three-nozzle form.
(R-R)

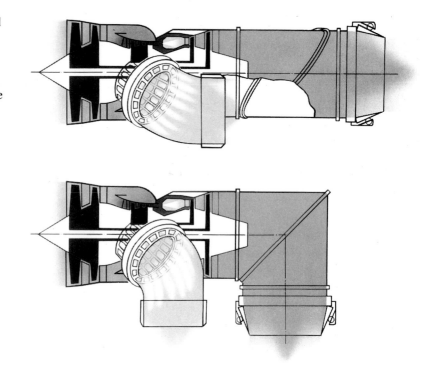

The RALS or 'bleed and
burn' system would take
compressed air from the
propulsion engine to a
PCB nozzle further
forward, this component
of jet lift being balanced
by deflecting the residual
thrust of the engine.
(R-R)

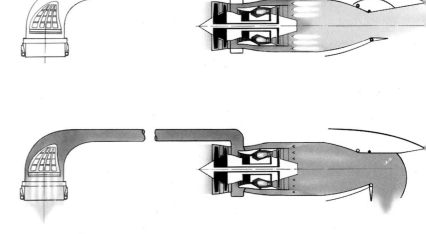

The ejector lift concept appears to differ from earlier augmentation schemes in that only part of the propulsion engine mass flow is diverted to the ejector, and the residual thrust of the engine is turned downwards. (*R-R*)

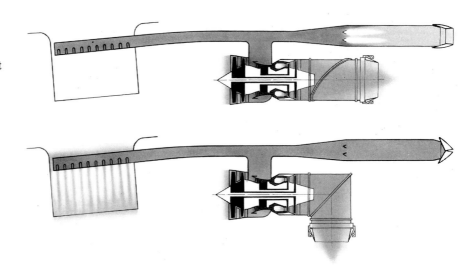

In the tandem fan concept the first fan stage is mounted remotely on a long shaft, and for jet lift all of the fan flow is deflected downwards by closing the duct. The second-stage fan is then supplied by means of auxiliary inlets, and the residual thrust is again deflected downwards. (*R-R*)

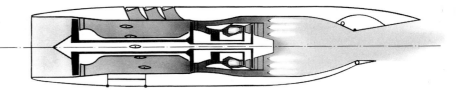

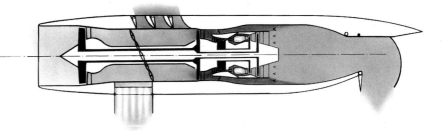

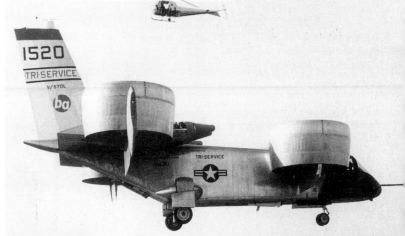

RIGHT Prior to adopting
the tilt-rotor concept as a
means to bridge the gap
between helicopters and
aeroplanes, the US tested
various alternatives.
These included the tilting
ducted fan, as employed
by this hovering Bell X-
22A. (*Bell Helicopter
Textron*)

This sequence shows tests with the Vought XC-142 tri-service tilt-wing transport, which was powered by four 3,080 shp General Electric T64s and made its first flight in September 1964. The aircraft was designed to take 32 fully-equipped troops or 8,000 lb (3,630 kg) of cargo. (*Vought*)

In order to optimize static thrust, Bell used ducted fans for the X-22A research vehicle, but it appears to have met with only limited success. (*Bell/Helicopter Textron*)

is believed to be studying a three or four nozzle vectored-thrust derivative of the PW5000 (YF119) engine, of approximately 30,000 lb (13,600 kg) afterburning thrust.

Osprey

The timescale for an advanced v/STOL fighter being introduced into service will eventually be settled by the useful life of the aircraft it replaces, which may well take IOC for the new aircraft into the next century. However, by the mid-1990s many medium-size helicopters currently in US military service will be ready for replacement, and this situation has led to a requirement for a v/STOL aircraft that effectively bridges the present gap between rotary-wing and fixed-wing designs.

At the end of 1981 the US DOD issued a requirement designated JVX, for a Joint-Service Advanced Vertical Lift Aircraft that would be used by all four services. In May 1986 Bell and Boeing-Vertol were jointly awarded a contract for the full-scale development of a project named the V-22 Osprey. The V-22 is to be a twin-engined tilt-rotor v/STOL aircraft with a gross weight of 40,000–59,000 lb (18,140–26,750 kg) depending on take-off mode, a cruise speed in excess of 275 knots (510 km/hr), and a ferry range of 2,100 nm (3,900 km), allowing it to be deployed anywhere in the world.

The V-22 is effectively a larger, high performance derivative of the Bell XV-3 and XV-15 tilt-rotor aircraft. The XV-3 first hovered in August 1955 and the XV-15 in April 1977. The latter project reached dive speeds of up to 345 knots (640 km/hr). The tilt-rotor concept was selected to fulfil JVX because it represented only a moderate risk, promised self-deployment capability, and offered considerable operational flexibility.

The resulting V-22 is a comparatively large aircraft, with rotors of 38 ft (11.6 m) diameter, although this dimension is in fact restricted by tip-clearance on LHAS (amphibious assault ships). It is powered by two Allison T406-AD-400 turboshafts of around 6,000 shp (derived from the T56), and is foldable for compatibility with carrier lifts. Advanced composite materials make up approximately half the airframe.

The full scale development (FSD) contract includes six prototype aircraft. Full production will be authorized in December 1991, when the first fleet deliveries will also take place. On initial plans the principal customer will be the USMC, which will have 552 MV-22A medium assault aircraft to replace CH-46Es and CH-53A/Ds. The USN, which replaced the US Army as executive service on the programme in 1983, will have 50 HV-22As to replace H-3s in the combat rescue role, but the service may also have 300 SV-22As for use in the ASW role, The USAF will have some 80 CV-22As to replace HH-53Cs and some special C-130s, also in the combat rescue role. Finally, the US Army will receive 231 MV-22As for use in the utility transport and medevac roles, superseding UH-60s, and CH-47s. Assuming that the US Navy goes firm on the 300 ASW aircraft, the domestic military market will represent at least 1,213 V-22s, with a peak production rate of 132 aircraft per year. Reports suggest the Army requirement may be increased to 301 aircraft. However, funding restrictions are expected to lead to cutbacks or procurement delays by all the services involved.

X-Wing

One of the alternative concepts that was turned down for the JVX programme, presumably because of the higher risks involved, was the X-Wing form of stopped rotor. The basic idea is that the aircraft may be able to take off and land like a helicopter, using a four-blade rotor, which for high speeds, is stopped to form one aft-swept wing and one FSW. However, in order to translate this idea into a

Precursor of the Bell-Boeing V-22 Osprey, the Bell XV-15 demonstrated the potential of the tilt-rotor concept. (*Bell Helicopter Textron*)

The Bell XV-15 in conventional wingborne flight. (*Bell Helicopter Textron*)

RIGHT This model-montage shows how the X-Wing would appear in high-speed flight on top of the Sikorsky RSRA (rotor systems research aircraft). (*Sikorsky*)

Cutaway drawing of the
Bell-Boeing V-22, showing
the connecting shafts that
keep both rotors turning
in the event of an engine
failure. (*Bell Helicopter
Textron*)

BELOW Prototype of the
Bell-Boeing V-22 Osprey,
pictured shortly after
rollout. (*Bell-Boeing*)

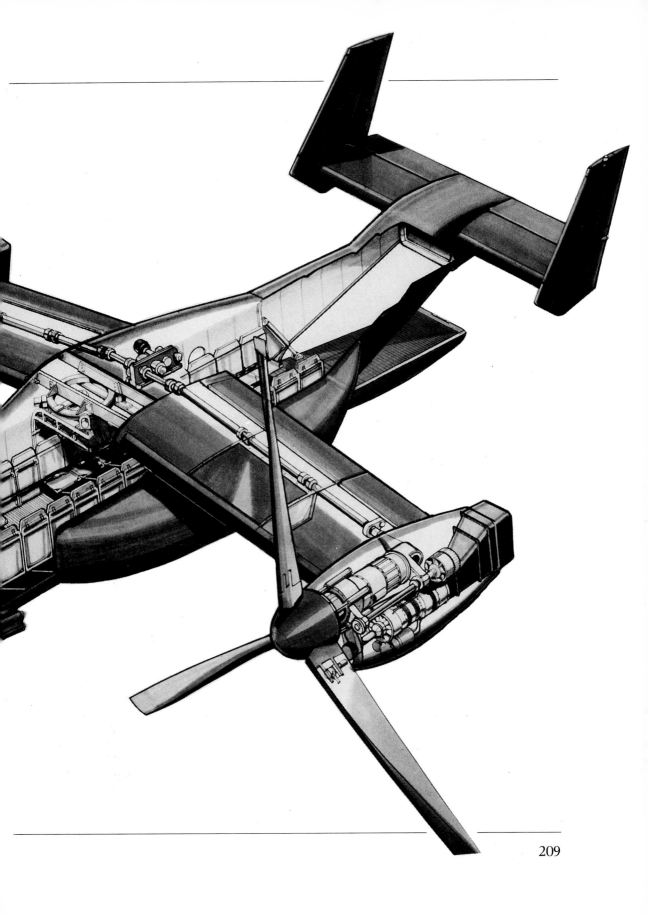

practical system, not only must the blades be extremely rigid, but they must also be able to create lift with the air approaching from either side. When the rotor is stopped, the leading edges of two of the blades become trailing edges, and vice-versa.

One way to solve the aerodynamic problem is to give the blades a symmetrical section (rather like two leading edges joined together) and supply high pressure air to ducts in both edges, which have slots to produce a jet-flap effect when air is supplied. The supply of air can be varied to suit the rotational or fixed use of the X-Wing, and it may also be modified to provide functions analogous to the collective and cyclic pitch controls of a conventional helicopter.

The feasibility of stopping and starting the X-Wing in flight is being tested on the Sikorsky RSRA (Rotor Systems Research Aircraft) under joint NASA/DARPA funding, although this S-72 is too heavy to permit vertical operation. The basic attraction of the S-72 is that it has a fixed wing of 370 sq ft (34.4 m^2), enabling it to fly and land without relying on the X-Wing to generate lift. It can thus survive complete failure of the 'pneumodynamic' (air circulation) system.

In its modified form the RSPA becomes the S-72X1, and is powered by two General Electric TF34-GE-400A turbofans of 9,275 lb (4,205 kg) thrust, with two 1,500 shp T58-GE-10s to turn the rotor and drive the two-stage axial-flow compressor that supplies air to the blades. The S-72X1 also has a blade-severance system and Martin-Baker ejection seats.

Rotor diameter is 57.6 ft (17.56 m), and design gross weight is 33,276 lb (15,090 kg). One evident advantage of the stopped rotor is that it makes possible the combination of a lower disc loading and a higher speed than the tilt-rotor. The disc loading of the S-72X1 is 12.75 psf (62.2 kg/m^2), though a more representative figure for a true X-Wing demonstrator would be 11.75 psf (57.3 kg/m^2). For comparison, the disc loading of the V-22 at VTO weight is 17.65 psf (86.1 kg/m^2), roughly 50 per cent higher. Likewise, whereas the tilt-rotor concept is felt to have a maximum speed of 300–350 knots (555–650 km/hr), it is hoped that the X-Wing will be able to reach 500–550 knots (925–1,020 km/hr). However, the S-72X1 is again not representative, having a predicted maximum of 300 knots (555 km/hr) with rotor stopped, and 200 knots (370 km/hr) with rotation.

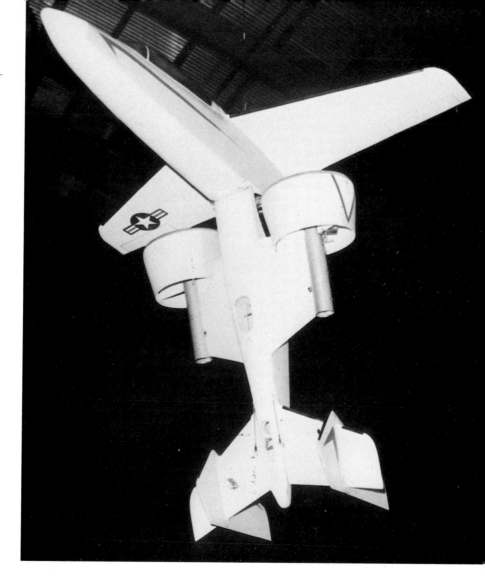

Yet another form of vectored thrust: a Grumman naval project with ducted fans mounted on an articulated fuselage. (*Grumman*)

An artist's impression of a Lockheed-California naval V/STOL project, using two tandem-fan engines with cross-ducting to maintain lateral balance in the event of engine failure. (*Lockheed-California*)

If no serious problems are encountered in flight tests with the S-72X1, then a true X-Wing demonstrator may be developed, with no fixed wing and with only two 'convertible' engines that will supply forward thrust, rotor drive, and power for the compressor that provides air for the jet-flap effect. This demonstrator would gross 24,000 lb (10,885 kg) and have an X-Wing of 51 ft (15.55 m) diameter. It would have full VTOL capability, and reach speeds of around 500 knots (925 km/hr).

Unfortunately, it is not clear how such an aircraft would fit into the US military inventory. The US Army has integrated its future attack requirement with that for a light scout and utility helicopter, the resulting LHX being a small aircraft of only 8,000 lb (3,630 kg) with a cruise speed of only 170 knots (315 km/hr). The IOC date of December 1995 could hardly be met by the X-Wing, and there are doubts whether such complex engineering is compatible with such a lightweight aircraft. The X-Wing would certainly produce a much faster vehicle than required by the US Army, which sees the LHX as a 'conventional rotorcraft'.

On the one hand, the US Army is clearly loath to specify an aircraft that would be highly expensive and that might well fall under the control of the USAF. On the other hand, it would be a great shame to see this idea go to waste, and there must be some fear that the Russians will develop it and dominate the air over the battlefield.

Summary and Conclusions

To recapitulate, serious interest began in V/STOL during the 1950s because of the threat of tactical nuclear weapons to NATO airfields. During the 1960s that threat lessened as NATO thinking changed form an all-out war to a graduated response in which nuclear weapons would be employed only at a later stage. Interest in V/STOL therefore evaporated in most Western air forces.

In the UK work nonetheless continued on the single-engine vectored-thrust concept, which led to the R-R Pegasus engine and the BAe Harrier series, and provided a starting-point for the second generation McDonnell Douglas AV-8B. The Harrier/Pegasus concept was technically successful, but had little success commercially, due mainly to its lack of supersonic performance and severely penalized warload-radius performance, its high unit cost, and half-hearted support from MOD and HMG.

Artist's impression of a Mach 1.5 STOVL fighter study by Lockheed Aeronautical Systems, funded by NASA. The design features a Rolls-Royce hybrid fan vectored-thrust (HFVT) engine derived from the tandem-fan concept. (*Lockheed*)

It is arguable that V/STOL development in the UK was in one respect decades ahead of its time, since lightweight composite airframes were desirable to make possible an acceptable warload-radius combination. On the other hand this conceptual lead was negated by the programme being consistently starved of funds: what could have been achieved in 10 years was actually spread over 30.

Vectored-thrust after 30 years of development is still lacking in some respects. Very little effort has been applied to PCB, which is an essential ingredient for advanced vectored-thrust engines. The development of a short landing capability at high weights by means of thrust reversal has received even less funding, although

The British Aerospace Sea Harrier FRS.2 pictured during its first flight on 19 September 1988. The Ferranti Blue Vixen radar fitted to the FRS.2 will have a look-down capability and will be compatible with the AMRAAM missile, making the Sea Harrier truly formidable in air-air roles. However, the next generation of maritime V/STOL fighters will need to be supersonic. (*BAe*)

the carriage of expensive weapons warrants this type of development.

Vectored-thrust is known to work in single-engined form, and there are no indications that this type of powerplant is unsuited to supersonic fighter applications. In these circumstances it is only natural that the UK should be biased in favour of further development along these lines. At the same time, it is worth keeping an open mind about some of the possible alternatives, including the use of two vectored-thrust engines side-by-side, as was considered in the 1960s for the naval P.1154. The RALS or 'bleed and burn' system may be also attractive in fighter applications. The old German concept of 'lift plus lift/cruise' engines produces minimum weight in the case of a strike/fighter, though it has always appeared somewhat dubious from a low speed safety aspect. Modern automatic controls for take-off and landing may make the tail-sitter or VATOL aircraft quite attractive in some applications, such as the point defence interceptor. For slower speeds, America is already developing the tilt-rotor and experimenting with the X-Wing.

It is painfully clear that the RAF has abandoned any idea of leading the world in V/STOL, because Britain's potential partners in Europe feel that there are significant and unacceptable performance penalties involved. The RN would like an advanced V/STOL aircraft, but will probably be obliged to wait until the USN replaces the F/A-18 at some time in the next century. If any serious development work is to take place on V/STOL aircraft in the West in the near-term, it thus seems likely to be done in the context of an F-16 replacement for the USAF, although even this is a long-shot.

Unfortunately for anyone advocating a change to V/STOL, the current USAF philosophy appears to favour advanced STOL concepts as illustrated by the ATF, with thrust-vectoring at the rear end for take-off rotation, and thrust-reversal following a precision landing. It may be noted that the Eurofighter seems likely to follow this route at its mid-term update. This form of advanced STOL performance is undoubtedly a vast improvement over traditional CTOL, but it is no substitute for V/STOL. The essence of the USAF approach is to estimate how much runway will be left after the Warsaw Pact has attacked a typical NATO airfield, and to combine all the established (mainly Viggen) measures to allow a relatively conventional aircraft to continue operations from this damaged base.

The drawback to this approach is that the runway length on which the whole concept is based is only an estimate of what will probably be available. If the Warsaw Pact concentrates efforts on a smaller number of fields, or if their runway attack weapons are more effective than estimated, then the residual runway length will be shorter, and USAF aircraft will be immobilized on the ground. The only way to remove the uncertainty is to be able to disperse combat aircraft away from the airfields. The only way to be absolutely sure that aircraft can continue to operate regardless of the intensity and effectiveness of enemy attacks on airbases is to adopt V/STOL. Whereas V/STOL in the case of a subsonic ground attack aircraft undoubtedly involves a penalty (since the former requires twice as much engine as for CTOL), in the case of an air superiority fighter the penalty is negligible.

It cannot be emphasized too strongly that Korea and Vietnam were phoney wars in which the risk of USAF airbases being

attacked was zero. In any future war in central Europe NATO airbases would be attacked both by aircraft and ballistic missiles, and possibly by cruise missiles. Dispersed sites are extremely difficult to find and individually represent low-value targets.

It is also worth emphasising that the location of the next major confrontation with Communist forces cannot be predicted. Instead of central Europe, it might come in south-west Asia or even in Africa. In these circumstances high priority must be allocated to operational flexibility, especially in regard to choice of bases. As demonstrated so convincingly in the Falklands conflict, in basing flexibility the V/STOL aircraft is in a class of its own.

As indicated above, the choice of powerplant concept for such an aircraft demands detailed studies, though this writer would like to see included a twin-engined vectored-thrust arrangement, which would be more acceptable than a single engine to some air forces and might provide scope for a naval derivative.

The Harrier/Pegasus combination has proved conclusively the feasibility of V/STOL, and there is now a clear case for extending this type of operation into the supersonic combat aircraft category. What began only as an interesting engineering exercise may now represent the key to survival.

An artist's impression of the radar equipped Harrier II Plus now being developed jointly by McDonnell Douglas and British Aerospace. Thanks to its multi-mode radar, the Harrier II Plus will have medium range AAM-capability while retaining FLIR if required. First flight of a development aircraft is scheduled for 1990 with fleet delivery in 1992. (*BAe*)

Glossary

AAA	anti-aircraft artillery	c³	command, control and communications
AEW	airborne early warning (radar)	CAM	(Conventional) Counter-Air Missile (Martin Marietta)
AFB	Air Force Base (USAF)		
ALCM	Air-Launched Cruise Missile (Boeing AGM-86)	CASA	Construcciones Aeronauticas SA
		CASMU	Consorzio Armamenti Spendibili Multi-Uso
AOA	angle of attack		
AST	Air Staff Target (RAF)	CG	centre of gravity
ASTOVL	advance short take-off and vertical landing	CTOL	conventional take-off and landing
ASW	anti-submarine warfare *Anti-Shelter Wirkkörper*	CW	chemical warfare
		CWS	Container Weapon System (MBB)
ATACMS	Army TACtical Missile System		
ATF	Advance Tactical Fighter (USAF F-22/F-23)	DARPA	Defense Advanced Research Projects Agency
AWACS	Airborne Warning and Control System (Boeing E-3)	DMZ	demilitarized zone (of Vietnam)
BAP	*Bombe Accélérée de Pénétration* (Thomson-Brandt)	DOD	Department of Defense (US)
		DSMAC	digital scene-matching area-correlation
BKEP	Bomb, Kinetic Energy Penetrator (Avco BLU-106/B)		
BOSS	Ballistic Offensive Suppression System (Lockheed)	FEBA	forward edge of the battle area

FLIR	forward-looking infra-red	LR-SOM	long-range stand-off missile
FSW	forward-swept wing		
		MBB	Messerschmitt-Bölkow-Blohm
GPMG	general-purpose machine gun	MDC	McDonnell Douglas Corporation
GPS	Global Positioning System (Navstar)	MRASM	Medium-Range Air-Surface Missile (BGM-109H/L)
		MSOW	Modular Stand-Off Weapon
HAS	hardened aircraft shelter	MUSA	*MUlti-Splitter Wirkkörper Activ*
HE	high explosive		(Fragmentation Warhead, Active)
HSA	Hawker Siddeley Aviation		
HZG	*Hauptzielgruppe* (main target group)	MUSPA	*MUlti-Splitter Wirkkörper PAsiv* (Fragmentation Warhead, Passive)
ICBM	intercontinental ballistic missile		
IOC	initial operational capability	MV	motor vessel
IP	initial point	MW	*Mehrzweckwaffe* (Multi-Purpose Weapon)
IR	infra-red		
ISO	International Standardization Organisation	MWDP	Mutual Weapons Development Program
JTACMS	Joint TACtical Missile System (USAF/US Army)	NASA	National Aeronautics and Space Administration
JVX	Joint-Service Advanced Vertical Lift Aircraft	NATO	North Atlantic Treaty Organization
		NBC	nuclear, bacteriological and chemical
KB	*Kleine Bombe* (bomblet)		
KHD	Klöckner-Humboldt-Deutz	NGTE	National Gas Turbine Establishment (Pyestock)
LAAAS	Low Altitude Airfield Attack System	OCU	Operational Conversion Unit (RAF)
LAADC	Libyan Arab Air Defence Command		
LAD	Low Altitude Dispenser	P&W	Pratt & Whitney
LERX	leading edge root extension	PCB	plenum chamber burning
LGB	laser-guided bomb	PGM	precision-guided munition
LID	lift-improvement device	PSP	pierced steel plate
LOCPOD	LOw-Cost Powered Off-boresight Dispenser	R&D	research and development
LOX	liquid oxygen	RAF	Royal Air Force

RALS	remote augmentation lift system	TABAS	Total AirBase Attack System
RE	Royal Engineers	TACEVAL	TACtical EVALuation (NATO)
RFA	Royal Fleet Auxiliary	TERCOM	TERrain Contour-Matching
RN	Royal Navy	TFW	Tactical Fighter Wing (USAF)
RNAS	Royal Naval Air Station	TMD	Tactical Munitions Dispenser
R-R	Rolls-Royce	TLAM-C	Tactical Land-Attack Missile,
RSRA	Rotor Systems Research Aircraft (Sikorsky)		Conventional (BGM-109C)
		TRAM	Target Recognition/Attack Multisensor
RTG	Raketen Technik GmbH	T/W	thrust/weight ratio
RVN	Republic of Vietnam (i.e., South Vietnam)		
		USAAF	United States Army Air Force
		USAF	United States Air Force
SAF	Swedish Air Force	USMC	United States Marine Corps
SAGW	surface-air guided weapon	USN	United States Navy
SAM	surface-air missile		
SCADS	Shipborne Containerized Air Defence System	VATOL	vertical attitude take-off and landing
SFC	specific fuel consumption	VFR	visual flight rules
SLBM	submarine-launched ballistic missile	VFW	Vereinigte Flugtechnische Werke
SR-SOM	short-range stand-off missile	VIFF	(thrust) vectoring in forward flight
SSM	surface-surface missile		
STABO	*Startbahnbombe* (Runway Bomb)	V/STOL	vertical or short take-off and landing
STOVL	short take-off and vertical landing	VTOL	vertical take-off and landing
		WW	World War
TA	Territorial Army (UK)	WOD	wind-over-deck

Index